Right Address ...
Wrong Planet

Children with
Asperger Syndrome
Becoming Adults

RIGHT ADDRESS ...
WRONG PLANET

Children with
Asperger Syndrome
Becoming Adults

616.89
08

Gena P. Barnhill

AⲀPC

Autism Asperger Publishing Company
P.O. Box 23173
Shawnee Mission, Kansas 66283-0173

2002 by Autism Asperger Publishing Co.
P.O. Box 23173
Shawnee Mission, Kansas 66283-0173

Publisher's Cataloging-in-Publication
(provided by Quality Books, Inc.)

Barnhill, Gena.
   Right address – wrong planet : children with Asperger syndrome becoming adults / Gena Barnhill. – 1st ed.
   p. cm.
   Includes bibliographical references.
   ISBN: 1-931282-02-1

   1. Barnhill, Brent. 2. Asperger's syndrome–Patients –Biography. 3. Asperger's syndrome–Patients–Family relationships. I. Title.

RC553.A88B37 2002   616.89'82'0092
             QBI02-200093

This book is designed in Lydian and Minion

Managing Editor: Kirsten McBride
Editorial Staff: Ginny Biddulph
Cover Design: Taku Hagiwara
Interior Design/Production: Tappan Design

Printed in the United States of America

TO MY SON, BRENT, who taught me to reevaluate my goals and dreams and to reflect on life's most important issues.

TO MY HUSBAND, PRESS, who encouraged and believed in me.

TO MY DAUGHTER, KRISTEN, who endured the tough times when we did not know what we were dealing with.

Except for family members, all the names of individuals in this book have been changed in order to preserve anonymity.

Table of Contents

Preface

The purpose of this book is to share our family's experiences and portray a picture of a young adult with Asperger Syndrome. All individuals diagnosed with Asperger Syndrome whom I have had the privilege to either meet in person or get to know about through their parents have their own unique stories. Our story is still unfolding as Brent finds his niche in this world. Although our family did not have the advantage of knowing about Asperger Syndrome when Brent was a youngster, we still had many positive experiences with teachers and professionals who cared about Brent and intuitively knew what strategies to use to help him be successful. Any mistakes or problems that occurred, as described to the best of our recollection in this book, were not caused intentionally, but were due to lack of knowledge, lack of experience working with individuals with autism spectrum disorders, and the unavailability of the diagnosis.

Now is an exciting time because we know more about Asperger Syndrome and children are being diagnosed and receiving support earlier in their lives. It is my hope that by presenting our story, readers can learn from our experiences, both positive and negative, and benefit from the lessons we've learned. The good news is that with earlier diagnosis and recognition of this syndrome, individuals can receive the interventions and services that will help them be successful throughout their lives.

– Gena P. Barnhill

Introduction

Many families can recall an Uncle Charlie, a Grandpa Harry, a distant cousin Joe, or maybe even a nephew who just did not seem to be able to socialize with others. Maybe he could not keep a job or held a job that seemed beneath his intellectual ability. He might have collected things such as railroad timetables, door-knobs, or pictures of telescopes. Perhaps this relative seemed a little eccentric because he talked incessantly about farm equipment, cement mixers, or some other rather obscure interest without noticing that his audience was not interested. In thinking back on family reunions, you cannot remember a time when he did not embarrass someone by saying something that appeared out of place or inappropriate, and yet he seemed to want to fit in and be part of the group. Some relatives referred to him as the "black sheep" of the family. You might have been fond of him or you might have been uncomfortable around him, but you definitely thought he was different, or perhaps odd.

I remember attending elementary school in the early 1960s with a boy named Jimmy. Jimmy was very bright in certain academic areas but just did not fit in with the other children and even appeared a little eccentric. He spoke loudly in a monotone voice and frequently blurted out inappropriate comments. He fixated on certain topics that were of no interest to the other children or the teacher, and did not seem to notice that he was boring them. He was often in trouble at school, and the class frequently implicated him in mishaps that probably were not his fault, as the rest of the class members were savvy enough to know who could successfully be implicated and blamed. My peers thought Jimmy wanted me to be his friend and teased me about that. I remember the dilemma of not wanting to hurt his feelings and yet not wanting to be associated with him because I wanted to be accepted by the other students.

It was uncomfortable being around Jimmy because we never knew what he would blurt out next. I now sadly wish I had been more of a friend to him and often wonder what became of him as he grew up. Given his behaviors, it's quite possible that he is now an adult with unrecognized Asperger Syndrome because this condition was not recognized in the United States diagnostic manuals until 1994.

Despite the recent recognition of Asperger Syndrome as a developmental disability, many educational and medical professionals as well as families are still unaware of this condition. Even if they have heard of it, they frequently do not know how to treat or intervene with the individual with this condition. Increasing efforts have been devoted to providing teachers and others with workshops and other information on how to provide appropriate interventions for these individuals during their school years. However, many older individuals have never been properly diagnosed with this developmental disability because the diagnosis was not available when they were school age. These individuals seem to be the "forgotten adults." Frequently, they have at least average intelligence and may have successfully navigated out of secondary school. However, college life or the work world was a disastrous experience for many of them, and they and their families frequently do not know why.

My husband, Press, and I have a 25-year-old son who was recently diagnosed with Asperger Syndrome. In fact, while I was taking doctoral coursework in autism spectrum disorders when Brent was 21, it became apparent to Press and me for the first time that Brent had Asperger Syndrome. Thus, began my quest to learn as much as I could about this condition to help Brent become a successful and fulfilled adult.

During my doctoral studies, I had the opportunity to work with many adolescents with Asperger Syndrome and their families in conjunction with several university research projects. The common themes I heard and learned about our children regarding their social, emotional, academic, and vocational lives, along with the impact of this syndrome on the family, led me to want to share our story with professionals who work with these individuals and with other parents. Despite some differences in the details of our stories regarding the search for diagnosis or the lack of support we encountered, and still encounter, there are amazing similarities in our situations and day-to-day life with Asperger Syndrome.

Through personal and professional referrals, I have received a growing number of e-mail and phone requests for assistance and information about adolescents and adults with Asperger Syndrome. It seems as though they are the forgotten individuals. Younger children are more readily diagnosed given the recent recognition of this disability. But parents of adult children did not have the benefit of knowing that the group of symptoms their child demonstrated was part of a developmental disability. Moreover, many did not have access to appropriate resources to help their children overcome the many obstacles they faced growing up, since no one knew about Asperger Syndrome. In addition, many of these parents experienced a range of feelings such as guilt, blame, or shame regarding their parenting skills prior to the recognition of their child's disability. Often they were made to feel that they were part of their child's problem instead of valuable assets in their child's life. Our experiences need to be put into writing so that other parents of children, adolescents, and adults with Asperger Syndrome and related conditions will not continue to feel alone and can seek help for issues that might be related to this condition.

Thus, the purpose of this book is to share our experiences and paint a picture of a young adult with Asperger Syndrome from a parent's perspective. Moreover, it is my contention that most parents know their children better than anyone else, and that their opinions and observations need to be valued and sought out by the professionals working with their children. I recently told Paul, Brent's psychologist during his elementary school years, about our recent recognition of Asperger Syndrome. We have moved to another state, so Paul had not seen Brent since he was 14 years old.

While a diagnosis of Asperger Syndrome was not available when he worked with Brent, Paul commented that most of the parents he has worked with over the past several years have been the best diagnosticians of this syndrome. They are able to supply a wealth of information to professionals regarding their child's developmental history and behavior, which would be impossible to obtain any other way.

We have faced many challenges before and after diagnosis, and yet one of our biggest challenges continues to be developing awareness in others regarding this condition so they can interact more effectively with Brent. The more information that is available concerning Asperger Syndrome, the more others can become exposed and thereby increase their awareness, and hopefully their acceptance, of these individuals. In addition to letting other parents know that they are not alone in their struggles by reading some similarities in our story, professionals may find these experiences helpful in understanding their clients and their families. When professionals meet frustrated parents for the first time, they need to not take this frustration personally, but realize that their client and his or her family may have been through many exasperating situations similar to the ones described in this book. Furthermore, adults diagnosed with Asperger Syndrome as well as those not yet diagnosed may find some striking parallels in their lives that they can share with others to assist them in coping with daily struggles. I believe that there is a need for others to be aware of the needs and strengths of both individuals with Asperger Syndrome and their families.

Part I of this book begins with our search for confirmation of Asperger Syndrome. The difficulty we had in finding a knowledgeable professional to evaluate Brent when he was 21 years old is not atypical. I just received a phone call last week from an adult who asked me where he could find a professional to evaluate him for Asperger Syndrome. He became convinced that he has been struggling with undiagnosed Asperger Syndrome his entire life after his child was recently diagnosed with autism. He and his wife sounded exasperated because they had already spent many hours on the phone trying to locate someone who could give him a recommendation for a knowledgeable professional. In fact, he had contacted several of the professionals I had talked to when I was trying to find a knowledgeable professional for Brent. One of them had recommended that he call me because I had been in the same situation. I cannot underscore enough how underserved and unrecognized these forgotten adults are. Therefore, I chose to begin this book with a description of our search for the root of Brent's difficulties. It is in the third chapter of Part I that some of Brent's early childhood experiences are recalled. We originally thought these incidences were isolated, but now realize that they are all part of what we now know is Asperger Syndrome. This information is important because the diagnosis of Asperger Syndrome is based on behavioral observations and developmental history. Perhaps others who read this can use this information to obtain a diagnosis and appropriate intervention earlier than we could.

Part II focuses on Brent's adolescence including school life, part-time work, and perseverative interests and obsessions. Part III highlights adult issues such as college years and dating, work challenges, again perseverative and obsessive interests, depression and anxiety, and navigating the social service systems. Part IV presents the perspectives of parents, friends, and family members of somebody who has Asperger Syndrome. In Chapter Eleven Brent describes the challenges he has faced and continues to face living with this condition. Press then discusses his viewpoint as the father of our adult son with Asperger Syndrome. This is followed in Chapter Thirteen by comments from other parents and family members of adolescents and adults with Asperger Syndrome. Part V concludes with a brief chapter on resources for individuals with Asperger Syndrome and their family members.

Although this book focuses on many of the challenges we have faced parenting Brent, there are many invaluable positive lessons to be gained from living with an individual with Asperger Syndrome. It is frequently refreshing and uplifting for us to look at Brent's reaction to situations he has faced that would have overwhelmed us and see him smoothly gliding through them. On the other hand, he often becomes stymied over situations that appear to be of minor consequence to us. At times, I wish I could have his perspective, so that I would not get so caught up in the nuances of navigating difficult relationships and challenges. He has taught us that there are other perspectives that are not necessarily wrong, but are just different. Because of Brent, we have been challenged to reexamine the meaning and purpose of our lives, as well as our goals and dreams. I thank Brent for the opportunity to reflect on life's most important issues.

– Gena P. Barnhill

PART I

CONFIRMATION OF THE DIAGNOSIS

chapter one

Recognizing
Asperger Syndrome

"**P**ress, please read these few paragraphs and tell me if this reminds you of anyone." I was sitting at the kitchen table with my husband and had just finished reading a journal article by psychiatrist Peter Szatmari of Canada describing the diagnosis, treatment, and outcome of a newly recognized diagnosis called Asperger Syndrome. This was one of the articles I had chosen to read to prepare for a research paper about this syndrome, which I had only recently learned about.

Working as a school psychologist for a local public school system, I was continually receiving referrals to evaluate and work with children and adolescents who did not seem to fit in with their peers and often frustrated their teachers by their behavior. These students did not clearly meet the requirements to receive the educational diagnosis of autism, and yet it seemed as though there was something neurological affecting their behavior. Linda, the school physical therapist, and I worked together on several child study teams evaluating some of these children. Although these children qualified for special education services, we both had expressed frustration that the current special education labels did not seem to capture all that was going on with these students.

Within a few months of this time, Linda and I found ourselves in the same doctoral special education class as graduate students with an assignment to write a major research paper.

Everyone in the class seemed to select a topic with ease, except me. Finally, Linda reminded me that I continued to question if some of the students we worked with might have something like Asperger Syndrome, so she suggested that I research Asperger Syndrome. Little did I know that what I would find out would touch me so personally and become the major focus of my life's work.

After taking several minutes to read the paragraphs I had marked, Press responded, "Sure sounds a lot like Brent." I was convinced that it described our 21-year-old son better than anyone had done before. Szatmari described a triad of symptoms that were the hallmark of this syndrome, including social and communication impairments that profoundly affect their development and the process of growing up. We knew that Brent experienced social skills problems that seemed to be more than just shyness. He did not have any long-term friendships throughout most of his school career despite his own desire to join in and our numerous attempts to orchestrate his involvement in school and classroom activities, the church youth group, summer camp programs, marching band, and Boy Scouts. Although he spoke well, he sometimes had difficulty comprehending verbal instructions. He also seemed to miss some nonverbal cues when interacting with others. Szatmari also indicated that these individuals have a restricted range of interests or a perseverative interest or behavior that permeates their lives. Brent was virtually addicted to the Internet!

This was the first time anyone had connected the three characteristics (social issues, communication difficulties, and a restricted, perseverative interest) we had observed in Brent together under one label. Brent had seen many professionals over his lifetime and had received many different diagnoses including neurologically impaired, perceptually impaired, learning disabled, attention deficit hyperactivity disorder (ADHD), depressive disorder not otherwise specified, anxiety disorder not otherwise specified, and possible atypical bipolar disorder. Although Brent demonstrated some of the characteristics of these diagnoses, he did not fit neatly into any one diagnostic category, leaving us wondering about what was at the root of his difficulties, until we learned about Asperger Syndrome.

I had reservations about sharing this new revelation regarding Brent's diagnosis until I had done more research on the syndrome. During my nursing school days in the early 1970s, whenever we studied a new disease or condition I became convinced that I had it myself or knew someone who did. I did not want to go through that again, and decided to continue to research the possibility of Asperger Syndrome before jumping to conclusions. However, my gut feeling was telling me that we had finally landed the correct diagnosis. Press agreed with the need for more information but for a different reason. He later admitted that he did not want his son to have this lifelong disability, so he convinced himself that he needed more proof before accepting this diagnosis.

Two weeks after the revelation at the kitchen table, Brent refused to take the medication prescribed by his psychiatrist to help stabilize his moods. Brent rarely dug his heels in, but when he did there was no moving him. Press and I became worried that he might be heading for a crisis episode similar to the one he had experienced less than five months earlier, which led to his first and only hospitalization.

We called Dr. McCartney, the private psychologist Brent had been seeing, to ask for advice. During this phone conversation Dr. McCartney said that he had been wondering if Brent might have a pervasive developmental disorder (PDD) that had never been recognized. Well, I then spilled all! I told him that I had been doing some research for a graduate school class and had become convinced from my readings that Brent had a PDD. In fact, more specifically, I thought that it was probably Asperger Syndrome. Dr. McCartney mentioned that he and the psychiatrist, Dr. Rubin, had recently been discussing Brent's case, and they both thought that Brent's learning disability had been contributing to his inability to express himself and process information and that further evaluation might reveal more specifically the areas of concern. Both doctors indicated that they wished this testing had been conducted while Brent was in the hospital.

We immediately agreed to pursue further evaluation. Moreover, we were able to convince Brent later that weekend to continue to take his medications by suggesting that he tell Dr. Rubin if he still thought that they were not helping him after he tried taking them a while longer. We also followed Dr. McCartney's recommendation and contacted Dr. Shapiro, a psychologist with experience in diagnosing neurological problems, to request an evaluation for Brent.

I am now convinced that most circumstances we face are not just coincidences. We are placed in these situations to learn something. Several months before I read about Asperger Syndrome, I had been asking myself, Press, and close friends to help me figure out why I chose to attend graduate school for the third time. I had told Press several years earlier to shoot me if I ever suggested attending graduate school again; and here I was back in a very demanding academic environment. But this time the whole experience felt so different. I became interested in learning more about autism because of a young girl I had evaluated and worked with as a school psychologist. I was on the child study team that first rendered the educational diagnosis of autism for her. As a result, I attended workshops on interventions for individuals with autism so that I could learn as much as possible to assist her educators and family in working with her more effectively. But here I was in 1997 in a very structured doctoral program that focused on autism and Asperger Syndrome. I liked my job and did not need a doctorate to continue my career as a school psychologist or to work with individuals with autism. So why was I in a formal doctoral program focusing on autism and Asperger Syndrome?

I did not know why at that time, but I now believe that it was to provide me an opportunity to recognize that although no one had yet rendered a diagnosis of Asperger Syndrome, we had been living with it for 21 years. The university I was attending was also the only university in the United States that offered educational course work specifically in the area of Asperger Syndrome. Coincidence maybe, but I choose to believe it was a divine intervention. Our family was to embark on a journey that would change the course of all of our lives and the course of my career.

Lessons Learned

Life is full of opportunities and divine appointments that are sometimes referred to as coincidences. These are opportunities for growth and enlightenment.

chapter two

Round One of the Search for the Diagnosis

When I called Dr. Shapiro's office, her secretary immediately put me through. As I explained what we were looking for and that we wanted to know if Brent had Asperger Syndrome, Dr. Shapiro quickly told me that I was at the right place. Furthermore, she could conduct all the necessary neurological testing and was familiar with Asperger Syndrome. She suggested I set up an appointment through her secretary to begin the evaluation as soon as possible while she got back to her therapy session with her current client. I was impressed that she spoke so readily to me, but I wondered how the client in her office felt about her talking to me during his or her scheduled time.

Brent had been tested frequently as a youngster and was not looking forward to another battery of tests. But he agreed to the evaluation, although somewhat reluctantly, and asked for the time off from work. We arrived at Dr. Shapiro's office sharply at the time we were instructed to be there. Thirty minutes later Dr. Shapiro and her assistant came to call Brent for testing. Brent later commented that the psychologist was late and had not even offered an apology. I thought this was an astute observation coming from the person with a social disability.

I completed some photocopied forms, including a behavior rating scale. Although I was concerned that some of the rating scales were designed for individuals much younger than Brent, I did not say anything. Instead, I read a book for several hours as I waited. Midway through the testing session, Dr. Shapiro came out and, in a very supportive and demonstrative manner, assured me that Brent was doing fine and that her assistant was now working with him. I frankly had not been concerned that he would not be okay since this did not seem like a scary experience and Brent had been through many similar evaluations during his school career. I began to wonder if I was supposed to be concerned, but chalked Dr. Shapiro's overly mothering approach up to possibly indicating that she was a nurturing person. Later, I wondered if this was a way to make up for being late rather than explaining why or apologizing. I had come along with Brent mainly because he had never traveled to this part of the city before, and he had a very difficult time finding new places.

When the first testing session was completed and Brent came out for a break, I asked him how it went. He said it was okay but a little boring. I also asked him about his time with Dr. Shapiro; he had only seen her for a few minutes and her assistant had conducted the testing. Dr. Shapiro's assistant told me that Brent did not seem to be motivated to take the tests and frequently needed to be coaxed to continue working. We were asked to come back for another appointment so he could complete the testing. It was also agreed that Press and I would hear the verbal interpretation of the evaluation results together several weeks later and that the interpretation of the results would be explained to Brent during a future session.

A couple of weeks later after Press and I had taken time off from work, we sat waiting for Dr. Shapiro to call us into her office to hear the results of Brent's evaluation. No apology was given when she arrived almost 30 minutes late. In addition, we were not given extra time to make up for the lost time for which we were charged. Dr. Shapiro began by telling us that Brent was a very nice-looking young man and that it was such a shame that he had these problems and struggled so hard to express himself. Her concerns were prefaced with a sympathetic shaking of her head accompanied by tsk tsk sounds. We asked if she meant that he had Asperger Syndrome. Her answer was confusing, so we questioned again. She responded by telling us that of course she was familiar with the disability because after all it was on the Internet! I am still not sure how that response was supposed to answer our question. Dr. Shapiro was good at responding quickly, patronizing parents, and changing the subject. The closest she ever came to rendering a diagnosis was to say that it seemed as if Brent had Asperger Syndrome.

During our session she accepted a phone call and spent several minutes speaking to the caller as Press and I sat anxiously waiting to find out more about Brent. I found this unnerving since we had paid dearly for this time. Moreover, I thought psychologists were only supposed to take emergency calls, not routine calls, when they were in session with clients. When Dr. Shapiro finally hung up the phone, she seemed rushed as she flipped through Brent's file, again remarking what a shame it was that he was so immature because he truly seemed like a nice person. Press and I did not find the frequent tsk tsk sounds and dramatic comments emphasizing the word "such" to be comforting. We wanted the facts! In other words, what results and information had she uncovered through this evaluation?

Press asked at what age she thought Brent was functioning emotionally. She quickly answered 11 years of age. When I asked why 11, she said because that was prepuberty. I then went on to ask if she could explain what had led her to that conclusion. Her response was that she could just tell. I asked about the projective testing, remembering that Brent did not think this had been done, and that Dr. McCartney had specifically requested this testing be completed. Besides, I thought this might have been how she obtained information on Brent's emotional status. In lieu of an answer, she flipped through his file some more and said it would all be in the written report that we would soon receive in the mail.

She then steered the discussion to treatment issues and said emphatically that Brent needed social skills training, which would be provided at her office. We agreed wholeheartedly that he needed assistance in this area. She then proceeded to say that one of her social workers would call us to set up the social skills training. Clearly, the session was over, and we were ushered out of the office despite all our unanswered questions!

The written evaluation report arrived several weeks after our exasperating meeting. It contained a two-page table of contents, one page of recommendations, and one glossary page defining the terms used in the report. My initial impression was that it looked professional and comprehensive. However, as I read the report closely, I realized that most of the information appeared to be standardized verbiage, probably used in many reports, with Brent's name occasionally inserted to personalize it. There was no mention of a diagnosis, which is what we had requested. Moreover, all the results were interpreted by comparing them to the results of the IQ score obtained during the evaluation, even though it was said to be an underestimate of his actual ability. Brent's three previous IQ scores, obtained during his public school years, were significantly higher than this one, so Press and I agreed that this probably did not represent his true intellectual ability. But then, why was it used to draw conclusions about his auditory and visual perception, and memory? If the IQ was an underestimate, these conclusions seemed meaningless! In addition, the report stated that Brent's measured IQ demonstrated relative strengths in auditory conceptualization, speech, and hearing and relative weaknesses in dealing with uncertainty. Knowing that IQ tests are not used to measure speech and hearing, I was confused. The neurological testing mainly consisted of some screening instruments and was a big disappointment to Dr. McCartney and us. The report stated that projective testing indicated that Brent felt secure within his family but tended to approach social relationships with caution and skepticism and had difficulty expressing his feelings towards others. No kidding! I had reported this information in the intake interview. We did not need to spend well over $1,000 to hear this!

Since Dr. Shapiro said that we could call her office any time we had questions, I called to get clarification on the report. Her assistant reacted in what seemed a defensive manner and did not address my concerns regarding the validity of the IQ test. She did repeat, however, that she had never seen anyone so unmotivated to take the tests as Brent. I didn't realize it at the time, but I now know that motivation or lack of motivation is a major issue with individuals with Asperger Syndrome. I think the lack of motivation should have been mentioned in the report instead of the meaningless IQ score that was not even thought to be accurate by the person administering the test.

When Dr. Shapiro returned my phone call from her car phone later that day, I asked her about the specific type of expressive language therapy she was recommending. She could not answer my question. When I asked if there was someone in her office who was qualified to do it since she had recommended that it be conducted in her office, she did not answer. I really wanted to pursue language therapy for Brent since he seemed to have significant problems in this area, but how do you look for therapy for a person who is 21 years old and appears to be speaking well? Certainly, the type of language therapy that I saw conducted with young children in the school setting would be insulting and childlike for Brent. Yet, despite the absence of articulation problems, he still had difficulties with language skills such as giving people clear verbal geographical directions to his home. I had also learned in my doctoral studies that difficulties with the social use of language is one of the principal disabling areas for persons with Asperger Syndrome.

But my main concern was the lack of a diagnostic conclusion. On the phone Dr. Shapiro said that it seemed as if Brent might have Asperger Syndrome. I then asked her to summarize her diagnostic conclusions for Brent's psychiatrist and psychologist as we had originally agreed. She indicated that she would mail them an addendum to the report. She further added that although he seemed to have Asperger Syndrome, his language was not quite like the language typical of individuals with this syndrome. When asked to clarify, she said his language was just "a little different." I was still very confused by the comment about Brent's language, since he spoke well but had trouble with the pragmatics or social aspects of language and with certain idioms and expressions, as is typical of individuals with Asperger Syndrome. When I repeated my request for clarification on how his language skills seemed different to her, she immediately responded that she had to hang up because she had arrived at her destination. Our conversation had come to an end after only three or four minutes, even though she had called me. I thought it was rather convenient that she ended the brief conversation when she did!

The more Press and I pondered Brent's language skills after our unsatisfying session with Dr. Shapiro, the more we realized that he had been exhibiting language difficulties characteristic of Asperger Syndrome as a young child that were not fully recognized by us or the professionals who worked with him. We had thought that some of the unusual comments Brent made were cute, never imagining that they were part of the constellation of symptoms or characteristics of a pervasive developmental disability. We fondly referred to some of his comments as "Brentisms." For example, he sometimes mixed up idioms or expressions. When he lost focus and appeared spacey, Press occasionally called him by saying, "Earth to Brent," when he was elementary-school age. One day around this time when Brent was playing catch with his sister, we heard him say, "Mars to Kristen" when she did not appear to be paying attention while he was trying to throw the ball to her – Earth … Mars … whatever.

We took Brent for a speech and language evaluation when he was six years old. We were told that although he had some weak areas, when all the scores from the testing were averaged, he fell within the average range of functioning. Later that year the school psychologist told us that Brent had trouble labeling objects, but he could explain their function and describe them. He did not qualify for language services at that time because this difficulty was not severe enough. This expressive language difficulty was never mentioned again by the professionals who worked with Brent.

As scheduled, Brent met with Dr. Shapiro to discuss the results of the testing. When he returned home from his brief appointment, he reported that she said he had attention deficit disorder (ADD). He insisted that she never mentioned Asperger Syndrome. Furthermore, he emphatically refused to see her again.

I called Dr. Shapiro to get clarification on what she told him. Yes, Brent was right! She repeated over the phone that she did not tell him about Asperger Syndrome because she said he would not understand it. I was livid! We were trying to be honest and up front with Brent throughout this entire process and she purposely deceived him! Press and I immediately agreed that she was the one who did not understand it, not Brent! We explained to Brent that we were sorry this experience had been so frustrating for him when the purpose had been to help more clearly identify his strengths and weaknesses. We never imagined it would be such an exasperating experience for all of us.

The one redeeming outcome of this frustrating search for a diagnosis was that Dr. Shapiro did send the addendum we had requested. It stated that Brent's symptoms of attention deficit were consistent with pervasive developmental delay and Asperger Syndrome and that these symptoms were not emotional, but derived from the neurological domain. It had been insinuated many times in the past that Brent's problems were emotional in nature, so it was a relief to receive confirmation that they were not. In other words, Brent's behavior was not a result of poor parenting or his stubbornness. There was a biological reason for his difficulties.

Lessons Learned

Being told that you are in the right place is not necessarily an accurate statement. Be prepared to keep searching for the right professional. Realize that not all professionals are knowledgeable in all areas, and do not be afraid to question their credentials and experience, especially regarding newly recognized disabilities such as Asperger Syndrome. Surprisingly, there are still many professionals who are unfamiliar with this developmental disability. Also, Asperger Syndrome is a neurological disorder, not an emotional disorder.

chapter three

Round Two of the Search for the Diagnosis

P ress and I wanted Brent to receive social skills training, but we did not want to use Dr. Shapiro's services. We had been working on social skills issues with Brent throughout his life, teaching him what to say on the phone, how to start conversations, and so on. However, he was still having difficulty and we were not sure how to help him.

I networked with people at the university and with colleagues at my job trying to find someone who was familiar with autism spectrum disorders (ASD) and Asperger Syndrome who could help us. Several times the best I got was, "Good luck. Let us know if you find someone who works with adults with Asperger Syndrome so we can pass this information on." One day a colleague suggested that I contact our local Regional Center where the Department of Mental Health is located. I found out that the Division of Mental Retardation and Division of Developmental Disabilities are considered part of the Department of Mental Health. I thought it was worth a try since Asperger Syndrome is considered a developmental disability.

I called the Regional Center intake coordinator, Ms. Steven, to set up an appointment to determine if Brent had Asperger Syndrome and if he could qualify for services to assist him with social skills and expressive language. She immediately suggested that we see Jason, because he was one of the psychologists most familiar with individuals with higher-functioning autism disorders, such as Asperger Syndrome. Moreover, the assessment was free!

Ms. Steven was familiar with Asperger Syndrome and spoke to me at length about how the Regional Center had been receiving an increasing number of requests for assessments to determine if children had an ASD. I explained that we had just spent over $1,000 on an evaluation that was inconclusive. Because I knew these same tests could not be repeated so soon, I wanted the Regional Center to know what Brent had already taken. Ms. Steven explained that she would be sending me an extensive form to complete regarding Brent's developmental history and consent forms to allow them to contact professionals who had worked with him. She apologized because we would need to wait almost three months to see Jason. I was so relieved that there was someone at the Regional Center who was truly familiar with Asperger Syndrome that I was not upset about the wait. In the meantime, the other professionals who had worked with Brent would have time to mail their reports and comments to the Regional Center so Jason would have all the necessary background information when we arrived.

The forms arrived at our home several days later just as Ms. Steven had said. I completed them, but had difficulty answering the questions in the small space allotted, so I decided to write a developmental history briefly describing Brent's first 21 years of life and attach it to the numerous forms. I wanted to make sure that I did not leave out any important information, and certainly did not want another fiasco as we had experienced at Dr. Shapiro's office.

Putting Brent's history down on paper was eye-opening! Press and I were amazed at the experiences that popped into our minds as we tried to recall Brent's past history. We recalled several events that we had forgotten about and that were painful to remember, beginning with his traumatic birth.

We had decided to have children about two years after we were married only to find out that I had some fertility problems and might have difficulty getting pregnant. After having an exploratory laparoscopy and being under a specialist's care for only six months, I found out that I was pregnant. Press and I were thrilled and felt truly blessed.

Our first child, Brent, was born after an uneventful pregnancy, but very stressful labor and delivery that began on Easter of 1976. Because the fetal monitor and amniotic fluid indicated Brent was in distress during labor, Dr. Bryan, the resident physician on call for my obstetrician that Easter night, decided to deliver him quickly with low forceps.

Brent's gray color, limp body, and lack of breathing at the time of delivery were extremely frightening to everyone in the delivery room. Dr. Bryan began screaming for help and for someone to resuscitate Brent. I had been working as a pediatric nurse prior to Brent's birth and knew that if he did not start breathing soon, he could suffer serious brain damage. Press, who had been a wonderful coach throughout the labor, was standing behind my head as we both watched in utter horror the panic and frantic attempts of the medical staff who were trying to save Brent's life. For several moments we both forgot about each other, engulfed in our own fear and sense of powerlessness as we observed the pandemonium around us. The nurse was yelling at me to continue to breathe into the oxygen mask for the sake of our baby's life. I did, because I felt completely helpless and wanted so much to do anything I could to help remedy this desperate situation. However, the intellectual part of me soon took over, and I realized that my breathing oxygen had nothing to do with helping Brent because the umbilical cord had already been cut. Brent was separate from me and was on his own fighting for his life.

After what seemed like an eternity, the pediatrician, who arrived after the emergency page for help, announced that Brent had a heartbeat. I asked how long his heart had not been beating, but they did not know because they had been concentrating on his lack of breathing and had not listened for a heartbeat until the pediatrician arrived. The heaviness in the room lifted when Brent began breathing and his color turned fairly pink after several very tense minutes. His Apgar score of 3 or 4 at one minute of life rose to 7 after five minutes. As an index for appraising a newborn's condition at birth, Apgar scores of 7 to 10 are considered good, whereas a score of 0 to 3 is considered extremely poor, suggesting the need for immediate resuscitation.

At this point, Brent was given oxygen and whisked away for a precautionary x-ray of his lungs and for monitoring in the newborn nursery. When the x-rays indicated that Brent's lungs were fully developed, the doctor told us that he probably would be fine and able to go home with me in a few days. No other medical tests outside of routine procedures were conducted, and Brent was discharged from the hospital after three days. This was the average hospital stay in 1976!

Once it was confirmed that Brent's lungs were fully functioning, the focus of medical interest centered on me – his recovering mother. Entourages of medical interns and residents came to visit to learn about fourth-degree lacerations that resulted from Brent's quick and forced delivery – a complete tear from the birth canal to the rectum. In the meantime, Brent was progressing nicely at the hospital, and the pediatrician did not express any concerns. Little did most of us realize that the traumatic events associated with Brent's birth would impact him for the rest of his life. All seemed well at that time. In comparison, his sister, Kristen, was born three years later under completely different circumstances. She cried immediately at birth and was a much more difficult baby to soothe in contrast to quiet, subdued Brent.

One comment from Dr. Bryan, who delivered Brent, came back to haunt me 21 years later. Before leaving, he said that he would be working as a family practice doctor at the military base where Brent was born once his residency was completed and would like us to consider seeing him for our family medical needs because he was interested in following Brent. When asked why he was interested in Brent, he said that it was possible that Brent's IQ might be 5 points lower given the traumatic birth. He never explained how he came up with the estimate of 5 IQ points, nor did he inform us that a possible loss of IQ points really could not be measured. When Press and I asked what he meant by his comment, he immediately reassured us that there was nothing to worry about because it appeared as though Brent would be fine. He just wanted to follow Brent's development. I remember thinking that what he said seemed odd, but there did not seem to be any need to worry. After all, we now had a wonderful, healthy baby!

Press and I were struck by what a physically beautiful and happy baby Brent was. He was easy to care for and slept and ate well. I remember my father commenting how fortunate we were to have such an agreeable baby. Brent had a very pleasant, soft cry, and only seemed to cry when he was hungry or apparently uncomfortable. My father said his cry sounded as though he was saying "la la la la," rather than crying. We all viewed this as positive. In retrospect, I wonder if Brent's cry would have been considered by the professionals to be undifferentiated and perhaps the first clue that something was not right. I also don't remember him demonstrating stranger anxiety between 5-12 months of age as most children do. We thought that he was a happy and agreeable baby. Unbeknownst to us, the very traits that we viewed as positive may have been foretelling of a more ominous future.

As mothers our natural intuition or gut feelings are more accurate than we sometimes allow ourselves to accept. I am now convinced that most mothers truly know their children better than anyone else, except maybe their fathers. I think we are sometimes distracted from focusing on the negative, or what we somehow know to be true, so we can cope and do what we need to during stressful times. For example, during my labor I knew something was wrong. I knew that I was bleeding, and I showed the nurse. She then called the head obstetrician at his home on that holiday evening to come into the hospital to examine me. He reassured us by saying that the placenta had started to separate but seemed to be healing on its own.

I later noticed dark pigment when the doctor broke my water. The nurse said this was nothing and quickly removed all the soiled bedding. I knew intellectually from my nursing training that this dark pigment was probably the baby's stool, indicating fetal distress. However, I believed her and was able to proceed through labor without thinking about it again and without medication. I think I needed to believe her in order to be an active participant in the birthing process. Later that evening after I expressed concern regarding Brent's heart rate, as shown on the fetal monitor, the nurses turned the monitor sound off, saying that they wanted me to concentrate on breathing and not worrying. They knew I was a nurse and therefore might be preoccupied by other professional concerns.

Just as I had put those fearful concerns out of my mind during my labor with Brent, I must have put Dr. Bryan's comment out of my mind, or at least pushed it back in the deep recesses of my mind, because I did not think about it again for years – not until I was completing the forms for the Regional Center. I was particularly reminded of how Dr. Bryan mentioned that he wanted to follow Brent's development. And now we were trying to confirm whether or not Brent had a developmental disability!

As I completed the forms and answered questions about Brent's development, I was reminded of his early years. Brent was a playful and adorable young child. He maintained eye contact and imitated and interacted with others. Friends and family commented on his pleasant disposition, his beautiful platinum-blond hair, and his big blue eyes. He reached most developmental milestones within normal limits, although somewhat at the later end of normal for walking and talking. He was followed medically by the group of pediatricians I worked for, and they did not have any concerns regarding his development.

His toddler years were relatively smooth. Concerns began to surface in preschool. He seemed to be jealous of his sister who was born when he was almost three years old, and at preschool he teased and poked at children in what appeared to be a way to get their attention. We sometimes observed the same behavior when he was with children in the neighborhood. Even though he was frequently reminded to use his words rather than touch others to get attention, this inappropriate behavior continued. However, we had not suspected that anything was wrong until his preschool teacher brought this behavior to our attention. Now it seems obvious that her astute observations were the first recognition that Brent had difficulties with social and communication skills that would persist and pervade the rest of his life.

Then came the questions on the forms asking about his school attendance and more specifics about when his developmental delays became apparent. As we completed the questions, Press and I were flooded with memories of Brent's elementary school years, which were traumatic for all of us. Now we realize that these difficulties stemmed from his social and communication deficits; however, the root of Brent's difficulties were not clear to any of us when Brent was young.

In fact, kindergarten at our public school was probably the most stressful school year. Brent's teacher had been teaching kindergarten for many years and had four teenage boys of her own. We were pleased he was in her class because she was experienced in dealing with children. However, Brent apparently was an enigma to her. He continued to touch other children while in line, typically was the last in line, and could not seem to follow the rules the way that the other children did. The term "impulsivity" was not used at that time, but in retrospect Brent demonstrated considerable impulsivity. Additionally, he continued to experience difficulty with toileting and had accidents mostly at home with soiled or wet underwear.

We went to school for our first parent-teacher conference in the fall of Brent's kindergarten year to be told for the first 35 minutes of the meeting how Brent was not fitting in the class. Finally, Press reminded the teacher that she had just spent 35 minutes telling us negative things about our son, and asked if she had anything positive to share. She was caught totally off guard and was not able to respond, not even to say that he was on time for school, had good attendance, was well groomed, or tried hard. Needless to say, we were devastated. Press and I had both been good students ourselves, and we naturally assumed our children would be too. We never imagined that we would hear our child was a problem in kindergarten!

The teacher recommended that Brent be tested medically to see if allergies were causing some of his behavior problems. So we spent the next several months going from one medical doctor to another and to a private psychologist in search for answers. But we did not receive any definitive answers. Brent did have allergies, but they were not thought to be severe enough to cause the difficulty he was having in school. In the meantime, we continued to receive notes from Brent's teacher on an almost daily basis indicating that his behavior was inappropriate and requesting that we punish him at home for his school behavior. Press and I did speak to Brent about his unacceptable behavior at school, but did not punish him for it. We believed that the consequence for his behavior at school should be given at school. After all, we did not ask his teacher to punish him at school when he misbehaved at home.

When we went to the spring parent-teacher conference, we were shocked to find the child study team there without any advance notice. The school psychologist, as a member of the team, asked us very personal questions about our home life after he told us Brent had mentioned in class that Ernie from "Sesame Street" had a penis. As we spoke, he began to take copious notes. It was very unnerving, and I felt as though my parenting skills were being attacked in front of a group of professionals whom I had never set eyes on before. In fact, they had not asked for permission to observe our son, which they did anyway. Furthermore, the psychologist commented that he could tell that I was a perfectionist. When he started his monologue on the Freudian aspects of Brent's preoccupation with Ernie's anatomy, I knew I was doomed. Doesn't Freud blame all mothers for their offspring's problems? It was at this point that I looked at my husband and the other team members and realized they were all ignoring the school psychologist as he rambled. It seemed as though there was some division or personality clash among the members of the child study team. The learning specialist appeared warm and nurturing and explained that we could take some time to think all of this over, while the school psychologist continued to ask questions and take copious notes.

Needless to say, we and the school team did not start off with a feeling of mutual trust and respect. In fact, Press and I were in a state of shock at the end of our supposed routine parent-teacher conference. As a result, we did not agree to allow them to evaluate Brent, and instead sought a private evaluation at our own expense. The private evaluation did not determine a diagnosis, but recommended that Brent might need individualized instruction at school. But when we contacted the school to request the evaluation they had so earnestly suggested earlier, we were told that it could not be conducted until the beginning of his first-grade year because it was close to the end of the school year, and the school team did not work in the summer.

On December 2, 1982, three months after first grade began, Brent was classified as "neurologically impaired" by the child study team in our local New Jersey school district. His elementary school years continued to present challenges, and we received many calls from the school and the child study team regarding his behavior. The school psychologist insinuated that some of Brent's behavior seemed to involve sexual issues. Paul, the private psychologist, told us that he did not believe that the incidents of concern to the school psychologist were sexual in nature, but reflected Brent's reaction to stress. Moreover, he contended that Brent had probably learned that some of his behavior was effective in causing a big reaction from the adults in his environment, given their responses in the past.

Press and I remained confused by the discrepant reports we received. Although family members did not see him on a daily basis as we did, they still commented positively on Brent's fairly even-tempered nature. Paul, the private psychologist, indicated that he found Brent endearing because at times he seemed so insightful, concerned about others, and intuitive. On the other hand, he commented that Brent had an almost innocent-like quality, was very naïve, and seemed to miss what was going on around him. The neighbor who watched him for 30 minutes prior to school each morning said that she sometimes felt that as if she was speaking to an adult when she conversed with him. One morning when she was arguing with her daughter over lying, Brent commented, "Barbara, she is not even giving you eye contact." Barbara agreed and began to discuss the situation with Brent. It was several moments before Barbara realized that she was talking to a nine-year-old boy and not "Siggie" Freud. This pedantic and adult way of speaking is one of the characteristics of Asperger Syndrome.

Around this time we also noticed that, although younger, socially Kristen was much more advanced than Brent. She introduced herself and her brother when they met new children on the playground, indicating that her brother was older but was shy. It was not long before we began having concerns about how Brent's behavior was affecting her. She was embarrassed by his reputation at school and let the teachers know that she was very different from her brother. Yet, the only diagnostic label that could remotely explain his behavior was that he had a learning disability, which was educationally labeled "neurologically impaired." However, his behavior continued to be different even from the peers in his class who were also labeled as neurologically impaired.

Also, during Brent's elementary school years, we noticed that he still occasionally experienced difficulty getting to the bathroom on time. We wondered why he waited so long to realize that he needed to get to the restroom. Other children did not seem to have this difficulty. At first we thought he was just too busy playing and did not want to stop to go to the bathroom. Press suggested that maybe he did not feel the pressure and urgency that results from a full bladder the way most of us do. Still we were baffled. How could he not feel what we all feel? Of course, we did not realize at the time that this was part of a constellation of neurological and sensory issues.

As I continued to complete the forms, I asked Press about his recollections of Brent's behavior, including obsessive and perseverative interests. We both agreed that his perseverative interests became very apparent to us during his late elementary school years. Brent became an avid baseball card collector at that time. However, no one realized that his perseverative and obsessive interests were part of the constellation of symptoms known as Asperger Syndrome. In fact, just 10 months prior to our appointment with Jason at the Regional Center, we explained our concerns regarding Brent's obsessive interests and social and communication difficulties in great detail to a psychiatrist, who was treating Brent following a suicide attempt. And even then, this classic triad of symptoms as a distinct disorder was not recognized by the psychiatrist.

When we arrived at the Regional Center for Brent's evaluation, Jason reviewed the forms, developmental history, and previous reports. He spoke with Brent and me regarding Brent's adolescent years, college years, work experiences, social life, hospitalization in May of the previous year, and his current functioning. Jason's empathetic manner was very encouraging and supportive and helped facilitate conversation with Brent. He told Brent that he could understand how difficult work and college must have been for him. Brent confided that he preferred working to attending college and that he was interested in hands-on or on-the-job training instead of attending formal classes. When Jason left the room to get some forms, Brent told me that he felt comfortable with Jason because he seemed to understand him. He also told Jason that he did not think Dr. Shapiro understood him the way Jason did. Again, I thought Brent had been very insightful to arrive at this conclusion.

Jason noted that the developmental and school history that I provided, along with our interview and previous reports, supported the diagnosis of Asperger Syndrome. He did not administer additional psychological or intelligence tests since he had Brent's records and recent testing results; however, he asked Brent if he could spend the rest of the scheduled intake interview time asking him some questions regarding his daily living skills and watching him solve some simple functional skill problems. In addition, he asked Brent if he could talk with me for a few moments alone. Brent immediately agreed.

Toward the end of our interview with Jason, he told me that he thoroughly enjoyed speaking with us and appreciated the detailed history. Actually, the history was condensed into three typewritten pages, but was expounded on in our conversation. Furthermore, he observed that Brent seemed to have difficulty with general conversation and displayed discomfort in this social interaction. He described Brent as demonstrating hesitations in speech, a somewhat blunted affect, and as seemingly missing interjections of humor. Although Brent sometimes appeared confused during the interview, Jason noted that he was easily able to be reoriented. Furthermore, when asked, Jason said that Dr. Shapiro was not widely known in the Asperger Syndrome and autism community, confirming my belief that when Dr. Shapiro told us we were at the right place, she was clearly wrong.

At the end of the interview session Jason provided us with forms stating that Brent had Asperger Syndrome and therefore qualified for services through the Regional Center. We would be assigned a case manager who would help Brent access any needed services. Brent asked for a male case manager because he had felt more comfortable working with male counselors in the past. We were assigned a dedicated male case manager who worked out of our local satellite office.

Lessons Learned

There are professionals who are familiar with Asperger Syndrome. You may need to be diligent in finding them by calling local resource centers, parent support groups, university programs, or by interviewing prospective professionals. The amount of money professionals charge for their services does not necessarily equate with the quality of their services. It is more important to determine if they have training in the field of developmental disabilities and experience with individuals with Asperger Syndrome. A detailed developmental history that expounds on the individual's social and communication skills and focused or perseverative behaviors is a critical part of the diagnostic interview.

PART II

ADOLESCENCE

chapter four

The Industrious School Years

Brent's transitions to junior high school and then high school were much smoother than the tumultuous elementary school years during which we experienced frequent calls from the school psychologist about one of Brent's impulsive moments or inappropriate behaviors at school. I remember feeling incredibly relieved that Brent demonstrated an internal motivation and drive to be successful at school as he transitioned to the upper grade levels. I had read a lot about children and youth with learning difficulties who had resigned themselves to failure and had pretty much given up trying to succeed academically. These youth usually became behavior problems, frequently dropped out of the educational system, and often became involved with the penal system. Fortunately, Brent did not travel that path during adolescence. While many teenagers were rebelling and causing grief for their families and teachers, Brent seemed to be trying to please his teachers and succeed in school.

Junior High

While we lived in New Jersey, where Brent spent the first nine years of his school life, his peers remembered his earlier difficult years and immature behavior, and several of them continued to remind him of these embarrassing times. One young man bullied Brent, especially when he arrived at his locker at the start of the school day. When Press requested assistance from the school counselor, the bullying at the locker subsided. However, bullies know when to prey on their victims and are able to find opportunities when there is minimal or no adult supervision. Lunchrooms, locker rooms, and the playground are often areas that can be problematic. We are not sure how much of the bullying continued unbeknownst to Brent because he did not have the intuitive skills that his peers had to navigate the social world. Brent frequently missed social and nonverbal cues, making him vulnerable to teasing and bullying.

On a positive note, Brent did well academically during seventh and eighth grade, and his special education diagnosis was changed from neurologically impaired to perceptually impaired, given his academic success and improvement in behavior. He switched classes each period, but his core academic classes were in the special education department. He continued to receive assistance in writing, as it was difficult for him to organize his ideas on paper. Penmanship was not targeted as an area of intervention, although his handwriting was and continues to be difficult to read. Our relationship with the school team had improved significantly since our initial contact eight years previously. The team ordered Brent's textbooks on tape to assist him with reading comprehension. Testing revealed that Brent could decode or sound out single words above grade level, but he was still experiencing significant difficulty comprehending what he read in books. This baffled the school staff at the time. However, now it is fairly well accepted that individuals with Asperger Syndrome can decode words at a much higher grade level than they can comprehend what they appear to read so well. Brent seemed to enjoy the novelty of the books on tape at first, but then stopped listening to them because he said that it took more time to complete assignments that way. Behaviorally, Brent seemed to be acting more appropriately at school. Fortunately, he never needed to be sent to the principal for discipline. This was particularly significant, given that Brent's elementary school principal moved to the junior high school when Brent did.

Brent obtained his first paid job as a babysitter for my friend's eight-year-old son when he was in eighth grade. Austin took the school bus to our home after school a couple of afternoons a week, and Brent entertained him until his mother got home from work. Austin was a very bright youngster who played chess exceptionally well. He always beat Brent, and yet Brent never refused to play with him. I remember thinking that Brent was a kind and compassionate young man as I observed him babysitting. Austin helped Brent organize his many baseball cards. They seemed to truly enjoy each other's company. In fact, Brent usually got along better with children who were several years younger.

High School

Academically, high school was a very positive experience for Brent. We moved to Tampa, Florida, prior to the beginning of ninth grade when Press received a job offer there. Although transitions seem to be particularly difficult for persons with Asperger Syndrome, moving from New Jersey to Florida in the summer of 1990 proved to be a positive experience, both socially and academically, for Brent. He was able to start over in a new school without the previous history of his school antics and misbehavior. He was enrolled exclusively in general education classes and did not carry a special education label. He seemed to flourish academically, and with our and his band teacher's coaxing became an active member in the marching band. This connection with the school marching band provided a safe and comfortable social environment, giving Brent a sense of belonging in the large high school community.

It was also during his ninth-grade year that Brent had his first official date. Brent's friend from confirmation class at church introduced Brent to Sue, a cute, petite girl who was one year younger than Brent. She was very gregarious and, hence, initiated and sustained much of their conversation. She very much wanted to go to the ninth-grade graduation dance, to which Brent asked her. Brent was so excited and nervous about attending this dance that he developed an upset stomach, which decided to act up in the car shortly after Press had picked Sue up for the dance. Luckily, Press happened to have a towel in the car that Brent was able to use and thereby prevent an unsightly mess. Sue sweetly told Brent not to be embarrassed because the same thing happened to her when she got nervous. Once they arrived at the dance, the evening went smoother. Brent had always enjoyed dancing and was not shy to dance. He was quite a good dancer, too! Brent was introduced to Sue's friends, and they all went out to a restaurant to eat afterward.

For several weeks after the dance Sue continued to call Brent on the phone and come to our house. One afternoon she called him up in a panic as her older ex-boyfriend was at her house and had gotten into her parents' liquor cabinet and was drinking their alcohol. She called back a little later to tell Brent that she was afraid that the ex-boyfriend might take advantage of her. After listening very patiently, Brent suggested that she call her father who was a policeman to help get this young man out of her house. Later he told us that he was not sure why she continued to allow her ex-boyfriend to come to her house. Furthermore, he was confused as to what she expected him to do and wondered if she wanted him to come over and rescue her. He said that he did not think he could fight her boyfriend.

Soon after that incident, Sue stopped calling and coming to our house. Although Brent was not sure why she stopped seeing him, he did not call her to find out. He told us that he would not be seeing her next year anyway because they would be in different schools. I was somewhat relieved that he was not upset about the breakup and also that he did not want to pursue this relationship. However, it was starting to become obvious that he was missing big pieces of the social picture.

Brent had to change schools at the beginning of his sophomore year of high school in Tampa because grades 10 through 12 were located in a separate building seven miles away. When Brent decided that he did not want to go back to band camp after attending the first long hot summer day, we contacted the band teacher at the new school to ask him to encourage Brent to continue. He seemed to have difficulty adjusting to new situations, especially when they involved large groups of new people. Luckily, the band teacher persuaded Brent to stay on, and he became a part of the high school marching band.

Brent did not display any behavioral problems in class and received good grades. He passed driver's education, but was reluctant to drive on his own once he got his driver's license. Although Brent had difficulty passing some of the academic tests, he was still able to attain A's and B's because of his good conduct, attendance, and willingness to do extra-credit work. He was busy with group band activities and after breaking up with Sue did not date again until he attended college.

Another job change for Press resulted in a move to Missouri during the last quarter of Brent's junior year in high school. Surprisingly, Brent seemed to adjust well to the move. Although we had only lived in three different towns during the course of Brent's school career, he had changed schools many times. We thought he was becoming adept at change. The school peers in Missouri were very kind to Brent, and he was included at the band table during lunch. Brent's good grades from Florida combined with his good grades at his new high school qualified him for the National Honor Society. We were thrilled for him, and he was proud of his accomplishment! We all thought that he had learned to compensate for his earlier learning problems. Nonetheless, Brent continued to have difficulty asking or initiating requests for help. However, with his perseverance and our coaxing and ongoing contact with his teachers, he continued to do well academically. Brent frequently completed extra-credit assignments to improve his grades because he sometimes had difficulty doing well on class tests. We did not need to remind Brent to get up in the morning for school or to complete his homework. He was motivated on his own to succeed and he demonstrated considerable determination.

Despite Brent's academic success, we still thought that he appeared to have difficulty focusing and maintaining attention to tasks, unless they were related to his current special interest. In that case, he could do nothing else but concentrate exclusively on that interest. I thought that he might have a form of attention deficit hyperactivity disorder (ADHD), although I did not see any signs of hyperactivity. His teachers had not voiced any concerns about his academics or behavior at school. Nevertheless, I shared my concerns with our family doctor, who recommended that Brent see a psychiatrist to rule out ADHD. The family doctor explained that he referred adolescents to a psychiatrist when ADHD was suspected and the diagnosis was not rendered prior to age seven. After interviewing Brent and reviewing all of his previous evaluations, the psychiatrist concluded that Brent appeared to have characteristics of ADHD. Brent was not hyperactive, but was experiencing difficulty with maintaining attention to tasks and with impulsivity. He began taking medication for his ADHD symptoms during his senior year of high school.

Brent became more interested in driving during the beginning of his senior high school year, but he was still nervous about driving. Once students were old enough to drive in Missouri, they almost never rode the school bus again. In fact, we did not know any students his age who rode the school bus. This was a motivating factor for Brent to begin driving on his own. When I bought a new car, Brent began driving my old one. Although he was a fairly cautious driver, we noticed that he sometimes missed cues as to what was going on around him, which worried us. For instance, he was driving to a class for College Board tutoring after school one afternoon when he sensed that something was wrong but was unsure what. He mentioned it when he got home that evening. However, I had already heard what occurred from a police officer who had called me at work to relay what Brent had done.

The police officer called to ask me I if I had a son who was driving a blue Ford Tempo heading west on Route 152 around 4 p.m. Instantly, an awful feeling of dread came over me. I thought the worst and assumed that he was calling to tell me that Brent had been in a terrible accident. However, the officer went on to tell me that he was furious with Brent and should have given him a traffic ticket, but he did not have the time to stop and do so. Instead, he had decided to tell me what happened so I could explain the gravity of the situation to Brent that evening. He must really have wanted to contact me because he tracked our home address and telephone number from the motor vehicle records using Brent's license plate number. He then called our home where Kristen gave him my work phone number.

In an exasperated tone the officer informed me that Brent did not appear to notice him for several minutes even though he was speeding at approximately 80 mph down the four-lane highway in pursuit of another driver, with his siren blaring and his red lights flashing. Then, instead of moving to the right side of the road, as all the other cars did, Brent moved to the center median. The police officer pointed out that he could have crashed into Brent and caused a serious accident because he was passing cars on the left near where Brent had pulled over. He was upset because Brent had been slow to react to the police car's imminent approach, and had failed to follow the established driving rule of moving to the right shoulder of the road when an emergency vehicle approaches with its sirens and lights on, indicating that they need to quickly pass. I explained to him that Brent was a new driver and assured him that I would explain the seriousness of the situation and make sure that Brent understood the driving rule.

Later that evening Press and I tried to explain to Brent what the police officer had told me. Brent seemed truly confused by the driving rule of moving to the right. He repeatedly told us that there were no cars in the left lane and that it looked safer and clearer to move into the unoccupied center median. We reminded him that he must have learned this rule in order to pass the written driver's examination, but to no avail. He said he knew something was wrong, but it still did not make sense to him that he should have moved into the right shoulder, which was already crowded with cars. We then drew pictures to visually show him that it would be unsafe and chaotic if drivers could pull over wherever they wanted when they saw an emergency vehicle approaching and explained that this was the reason the rule was established.

Brent's teen years provided more positive reinforcement than his earlier years, especially in school. In hindsight, now that we know that Asperger Syndrome is a developmental disability, it makes sense that Brent was probably socially and emotionally experiencing what individuals several years younger go through, rather than the tumultuous and rebellious adolescent years that his peers were going through. These years would soon follow when Brent reached early adulthood, however.

Part-Time Jobs

Prior to the diagnosis of Asperger Syndrome, Brent had several part-time and summer jobs in high school and college. His first job in May of 1993 was as a sacker at our local supermarket during the end of his junior year in high school. This was a typical high school part-time job in our area of the country. Brent put groceries into plastic or paper sacks for customers as the cashier checked out their groceries, assisted customers to their cars, unloading the groceries into their cars if they needed help. In addition, he gathered grocery carts from the parking lot and brought them into the supermarket, stocked items for the dairy department, and performed miscellaneous cleaning tasks as requested by the manager. One of the managers, Lon, took an interest in Brent by praising him and expressing appreciation regarding his efforts.

As a result, Brent seemed to want to please him by carrying out any task that he was asked to complete.

During this time, Press and I continued to positively reinforce Brent for his success at work and at school while explaining the responsibilities of being a good employee. He did not seem to intuitively know that he needed to be on time, check his schedule every week because it changed weekly, notify his manager if he had a scheduling conflict, and call in sick if he did not feel well. We explained why these were important behaviors and he complied, but he still did not seem to really know why they were so significant. We did not want to hover over him and constantly supervise him, and yet we were afraid to back away completely for fear that he would lose his job for infractions of the work rules.

At the time we thought his difficulties in planning and remembering were due to attentional difficulties and possibly ADHD. We now realize that Brent was not able to easily consider these rules from a perspective other than his own due to his undiagnosed neurological condition. This difficulty with perspective taking is called a "theory of mind" deficit in the research literature. Researchers such as Ozonoff and Miller (1995) have defined this as the individual's inability to infer the mental states of others such as their knowledge, intentions, beliefs, and desires. By age 4, typically developing children usually begin to understand that other people have thoughts, knowledge, and beliefs that will influence their behavior. According to Attwood (1998) and Baron-Cohen and colleagues (1997), people with Asperger Syndrome seem to have difficulty conceptualizing and appreciating the thoughts and feelings of others. The degree of theory of mind deficits varies among individuals with Asperger Syndrome. Of course, none of us was aware that Brent had this condition at that time!

Press and I were also baffled by Brent's inability to intuitively figure out and understand the rules of conduct as an employee. We just seemed to pick these rules up on our own without any formal instruction and naturally assumed everyone else did. That is, everyone except Brent! Several years later when Kristen began her first part-time job, she also intuitively picked up the unwritten social rules. However, we now know that part of Brent's struggle also involved a lack of understanding what is sometimes referred to as the "hidden curriculum," rules that everyone seems to know but that are not formally written down or necessarily spoken. These rules often vary in different environments. For example, it may not be overtly stated but most workers know that one of their supervisors will tolerate an employee being a few minutes late to work but will not tolerate a messy work area. On the other hand, another supervisor will not tolerate tardiness, but does not care how the work area looks. These preferences are not written down, but everyone just recognizes them after working some place for a while. Lack of understanding of these subtle rules is characteristic of individuals with Asperger Syndrome. Brent was not the only person experiencing these difficulties, but we did not know anyone else at the time with similar struggles.

Brent experienced success as a sacker with the support of us and his manager. Lon was willing to be flexible and overlook some of Brent's weaknesses. Press spoke to Lon several times, thanking him for the positive attention he gave Brent and for the flexibility he provided regarding his work schedule. Press did not want Brent to work more than two evenings during the week, but to put in most of his scheduled hours on the weekend when there was no school. Lon tried to respect this wish as much as possible. Lon, in turn, told us that he liked Brent and that he was a good worker. Brent continued to work at the supermarket until he left for college in August of 1994.

Lessons Learned

We did not realize that the industrious teen years were a delayed developmental stage that would soon lead to a difficult and unsettling period during young adulthood. However, this relatively smooth academic time provided a lot of positive reinforcement for Brent, whereas his elementary school years were fraught with failure and conflict. It would have been helpful to know that Brent had Asperger Syndrome so appropriate social skills interventions and manipulation of the academic environment could have been implemented to increase opportunities for successful experiences throughout Brent's school career. His academic strengths (e.g., word decoding) and weaknesses (e.g., reading comprehension, penmanship) also make sense now in light of the diagnosis of Asperger Syndrome.

We recently found out from other parents of adult children with Asperger Syndrome that it is fairly common for these teens to feel hesitant about driving, and many delay obtaining their driver's license. In addition, social awkwardness often contributes to delayed dating for many as it did for Brent.

References

Attwood, T. (1998). *Asperger's syndrome.* London: Jessica Kingsley.

Baron-Cohen, S., Jolliffe, T., Mortimore, C., & Robertson, M. (1997). Another advanced test of theory of mind: Evidence from very high functioning adults with autism or Asperger Syndrome. *Journal of Child Psychiatry and Psychology, 38,* 813-822.

Ozonoff, S., & Miller, J. (1995). Teaching theory of mind: A new approach to social skills training for individuals with autism. *Journal of Autism and Developmental Disabilities, 25,* 415-433.

chapter five

Idiosyncrasies

We did not have a label for Brent's very focused behavior during his adolescent years; however, we now know that he was demonstrating perseverative behavior characteristic of Asperger Syndrome. Our first recognition of this intense behavior occurred when Brent was about 10 years old. He started buying wax packs of baseball cards with his allowance and gift money. He then began reading the baseball collector's magazines to determine the value of his cards. We were thrilled that Brent wanted to read because up until this point he never read for enjoyment because his reading comprehension was so poor. During his intense baseball card-collecting phase, most of his reading involved statistics rather than words. Nevertheless, it was encouraging to see him recognize the usefulness of reading and initiate reading about baseball to increase his knowledge.

Within a short time, Brent became obsessed with collecting baseball cards. In retrospect, this hobby had some of the characteristics of a gambling addiction. For $.50 Brent could buy approximately seven cards and a small stick of bubble gum sealed in a wax pack. Sometimes the cards had little or no value, but at other times they were worth $1 or $2. He never knew what cards he would get; the excitement was in finding out if he got a valuable card. Furthermore, there was also the chance that one of the Rookie cards he got would turn out to be valuable if the baseball player depicted became a star. In essence, the collector never knew if a card would turn out to be valuable at some point in time. Of course, there also was the possibility that he would get a card that was currently valuable.

Brent asked us to take him to baseball card shows where he could buy single cards that were priced less than the value stated in the magazine price guides. He began purchasing cards that he was missing to make a complete set of 792 cards. Brent methodically checked the local newspaper, baseball card magazines, and the magazine price guide to find out when baseball card shows were scheduled, because he did not want to miss a chance to purchase a needed card. One time Press purchased a whole case of unsorted cards for Brent's birthday from an adult acquaintance who sold baseball cards. Brent poured over the cards for hours each day, sorting them into sets. Each case produced 10-12 complete sets with several thousand miscellaneous cards left over. After receiving the first case of unsorted cards, Brent was hooked! He used all his money to purchase unsorted cases of baseball cards. He even thought that he would go into business for himself and sell the sets he sorted at a profit. But after selling two sets of cards to friends, he could not part with the cards and decided to add them to his growing collection. He even enlisted Austin's help to sort the cards when he babysat after school.

After returning from a flea market one day, Brent showed me a card with Mickey Mantle's picture and a green signature. He was very excited because his price guide indicated that this signed card was one of a limited number that Mickey Mantle had signed for a commemorative series. I thought that Brent was being naïve and that the card was machine signed, not hand signed as he insisted. To resolve the matter, Press took Brent and the card to a baseball card dealer where they found out that it was indeed worth quite a bit of money. In fact, the dealer offered to buy the card for $600.

Brent's baseball card fever increased significantly after this positive reinforcement! He continued to remind us that he only paid $.50 for the wax pack of cards and had by chance obtained a card worth between $600 and $1,200. One day he obtained another Mickey Mantle card – this time machine signed.

Even though Brent had done quite a bit of reading and knew the magazine value of many baseball cards, he had been taken advantage of by peers who were more savvy at the art of negotiating. Several months earlier, Brent had been so excited about trading cards that he was unaware that a peer had taken advantage of him until the transaction was over. Brent realized that it was an extremely unfair exchange and was very upset when he arrived home. Press became equally upset that a peer would take advantage of Brent, so he went to his house to talk to the parents and to ask for the card back. He was able to get the card back, but remarked to me that he felt very uncomfortable having to speak to the boy's father about the situation. Press was embarrassed that Brent was not able to negotiate and had allowed the boy to take obvious advantage of him.

Brent finally agreed to put the Mickey Mantle cards into a safety deposit box as we had asked him earlier. He had already been storing these cards in special cases so they would not get damaged. For the card to be worth the magazine value, it had to be in mint condition. Brent later traded the machine-signed Mickey Mantle at a baseball card show for $35 worth of other cards that he wanted. He was in a frenzy now, buying and trading cards. Several times he asked us if he could trade the signed Mickey Mantle card for other cards that he wanted but Press was able to talk him out of it. Not having immediate access to the card probably helped. Press also explained to Brent that the card was an investment and should be put away and saved in case it became very valuable in the future. That card is still in our safety deposit box.

Approximately five years later, Brent abruptly announced that he no longer was interested in collecting baseball cards and wanted to get rid of all of them. He did not know why; he just knew that he was not interested in collecting any more. By this time he had amassed over 40,000 cards! Press talked him into storing them for a while, in case he became interested again or if in the future he wanted to pass them on to his children. Brent did not look at cards again for about nine years, when he briefly began collecting again. But now a wax pack of cards cost three times more, and he could not afford to continue buying them. It was at this time in Brent's life that we realized he had a proclivity toward addictive behavior.

We noticed that Brent was very organized in certain areas of his life, yet very disorganized in others. For example, he would get up in the morning for junior high school in plenty of time to get ready for school, but then would start watching television and invariably end up rushing around at the last second to catch the school bus in time. To help him better organize his time, I suggested that he make a morning schedule. He agreed and immediately posted a schedule over his bed that detailed his morning minute by minute. I was very surprised to say the least! I had envisioned a schedule that would be divided into maybe 10- or 15-minute increments, not minute-by-minute intervals of time. I remember thinking that his response to my suggestion to make a schedule was a bit excessive, but I did not think about it again until we learned about Asperger Syndrome and realized that this behavior was probably part of the syndrome.

We also observed that without being asked, Brent would thoroughly clean his room, clothes closet and dresser every few months. I did not think this was too unusual, because I also liked to do a thorough cleaning once or twice a year. Once he decided that he did not want a toy or some other item in his room any more, he simply threw it in the garbage. Since we found that he sometimes threw out items that we considered valuable or at least worthy of keeping, I started to ask to see what he wanted to throw out first, in case we could donate the items or clothing to a charity. He agreed, so every few months a mound of clothing and other items would appear on the floor right outside his room. He did not ask if we were having company over to visit or if it was inconvenient for the castaway items to be cluttering the hallway. He just wanted his room to be tidy and organized. I think this gave him a feeling of being orderly and in control of his environment.

Around this time Brent became very interested in learning about sex and the physical changes males and females undergo as they develop into adults. This interest was appropriate for persons his age, but again his interest seemed a bit excessive. We spoke to him about sex and bought a book that clearly explained the changes young people go through. Brent was probably thinking the same things as other adolescent boys, but the difference was that he would openly talk about his thoughts and questions instead of keeping them to himself. His comments frequently embarrassed Kristen, who let us know about Brent's inappropriate remarks. For example, when shopping at a department store one day, he asked Kristen if she wanted to look at the bras. He continued to pour over books to learn as much as possible. He even began typing outlines of what he had read onto the computer each day. I explained that although he found this information fascinating, others might think it inappropriate if he discussed it in public. I tried to explain to him what was socially appropriate to talk about and what was not. I remember being confused as to why this was so difficult for Brent to learn and understand. Brent promised me that he would only share this type of information at home, but I remember having to signal him several times to stop in mixed company.

Later Brent began studying nutrition from my nursing nutrition book and from Internet sites. Again, he took copious notes and typed numerous pages of detailed outlines about what he had read. He seemed fascinated with isolated facts or tidbits of information, but he did not actually change his eating habits to a healthier style as a result of what he read. As is typical with many individuals with Asperger Syndrome, he could memorize the facts, but had difficulty applying them.

Although Brent continued to do well academically, I remember wishing that he would study for his classes with the intensity and organization that he did when he was pursuing a perseverative interest. We suggested that Brent write note cards and then repeat out loud what he wrote to help him study and memorize information for tests at school. This would provide him with a visual, auditory, and kinesthetic approach to learning. He thought we were crazy and refused, saying it would take too much time. He seemed to rely mostly on his memory to pass academic tests and found it difficult to study from notes. Again, I found it confusing that he seemed to have the skills to study intensely, but only used them to study certain narrow topics of interest.

In hindsight, I recall that Brent demonstrated a few other idiosyncratic behaviors that did not appear to be too excessive, but probably also were part of the syndrome. Brent was a relatively hearty eater until he developed some food preferences, but they seemed to be typical compared to peers. However, whenever we would go out to a restaurant during his early adolescent years, he could not eat if there was a young girl nearby. This would happen even if he did not have a crush on the girl. This phase eventually passed, and he was fortunately able to eat when he later went on dates. He also experienced a brief time when he could not eat at home if the cat was sitting on the floor next to him. He could not explain why, except to say that it turned him off and that he did not like the cat to be in the same room when he ate.

Brent also experienced some mild sensory issues that have continued into adulthood. For instance, he still sleeps in a cocoon, tightly wrapped in his sheets and blankets no matter how hot the temperature. If it is very hot, he turns on an oscillating fan that blows on him throughout the night. He probably finds the tightness of the blankets comforting, even though he sometimes gets overheated and becomes nauseous.

Lessons Learned

Unknown to us, Brent's obsessive-like behavior is one of the defining characteristics of Asperger Syndrome, namely, a perseverative interest or ritualistic behavior. When Brent developed an interest, he pursued it with intense zeal, and when he was no longer absorbed, the interest stopped with no warning and was replaced by another interest. In addition, his inability to intuitively pick up social skills is another major characteristic. Before his diagnosis, we thought that he was shy and that our parenting skills might have contributed to his difficulties. After talking with other parents of children with Asperger Syndrome, I have found that this is a common parental fear and that dedicated and responsible parents tend to blame themselves and question their parenting skills. What a relief to now know that Asperger Syndrome is a neurological condition and is not caused by poor parenting! However, I am convinced that an early diagnosis is important so the appropriate interventions can be implemented to help these individuals be successful academically and socially.

PART III

ADULT ISSUES

Due to the lifelong, often devastating impact of Asperger Syndrome, I have elected to discuss some of the major areas affecting Brent out of chronological order. The result is that you will find some repetition and leaps in time, but I feel that a more focused discussion of such areas as anxiety, sexuality, depression, work-related issues, obsessions, and so forth, merit such minor inconvenience.

– Gena P. Barnhill

chapter six

College Years and Dating

Three months after graduating from high school and receiving a small scholarship, Brent began college 95 miles from home. He was accepted based on his high school academic average and his Math College Board scores. His English College Board scores were weak, suggesting that he might need additional tutoring or assistance. I was hoping that he would be able to get this help and not feel overwhelmed on the university campus, which was not large but certainly much bigger than his high school campus.

We followed Brent to school in our minivan prior to freshman orientation, so we could help bring the clothes, small refrigerator, and essential supplies he needed to begin his new life away from home. He had been looking forward to this day for some time just as we had. I did not realize that I would feel so sad when he left home and was caught off guard by feelings of loss and concern as we left the campus to drive home. The reality that he was actually moving toward adulthood and might never live at home again really hit me!

Brent was quiet, but he seemed fine as we prepared to leave the campus for the drive home. Even though he had always been fairly quiet and shy, I still worried about leaving him alone. We had lunch with him earlier at the university, so we knew that he could find his way to the cafeteria. However, I wondered if he might eat alone and not have somebody to eat with. Brent knew that some other students from his high school were attending the university too, but he did not know them personally.

Brent briefly met his roommate, Al, a 22-year-old man from Turkey, who had arrived earlier because a longer orientation was required for the international students. We had been expecting another 18-year-old roommate and were not sure how rooming with a 22-year-old from the other side of the world was going to work out for Brent, who had led a rather sheltered life and was not very worldly.

When we got home, we decided not to phone Brent until he called us, because we did not want to seem overprotective or smothering. After several days had gone by and we still had not heard from Brent, I asked Press if he thought it would be okay to call him. I did not want Brent to think that we were worried or questioned his ability to live independently. I intended to act nonchalant and just ask him how things were going. It was after 11 a.m. when I finally called. To my surprise, a bubbly, young woman answered the phone. She indicated that Brent was still sleeping. Brent lived in an all-male, high-rise dorm. I don't know if the young woman picked up on my surprise, but she immediately explained that she was his roommate's friend and that Al let her use the computer in their room when he was in class. She was busy using the computer when I called. When I spoke to Brent, he acted very matter of fact about her and said that she was often in their room, but that did not bother him. She was very friendly and was also showing him how to use the computer.

Freshman Year

Two weeks after school began, Brent came home to spend Labor Day weekend with us. My cousin Dawn from Florida was also visiting that holiday. Dawn and I were sitting in the family room when Brent arrived. He walked into the room with his head held high and his shoulders back, looking very confident and poised. This was not the posture or demeanor Brent typically exhibited – usually he walked with slightly slumped shoulders. He looked like a new man! Dawn commented on how happy and mature he looked, to which he responded that he was going on a date that night with a 20-year-old woman he had met on the Internet. Dawn, who was single, jokingly asked Brent if he had any dating tips for her since it had been a while since she had dated. "It's easy," he said, "you just have to get aggressive with your words." He was referring to his typewritten words, also referred to as chatting on the Internet. Brent's humor can be very enchanting and sometimes catches you off guard. However, I think he was being serious when he responded to Dawn.

Brent had never written much for pleasure before he arrived at college. Writing had been a laborious chore for him, which he consequently avoided whenever possible. However, since arriving at college, he had spent a considerable amount of time writing to young women on the Internet and found that writing could be a pleasurable pastime. Since reading comprehension and writing had always been challenging for Brent, it was good to see him taking an interest in developing these skills. Of course, having internal motivation to do so really helped! Obtaining dates also positively reinforced his writing and chatting on line. I now realize that chatting or writing messages to others via the Internet can be an effective way to communicate with others when you have Asperger Syndrome. The otherwise awkward silent pauses in conversation that are common to individuals with Asperger Syndrome are not obvious when you are typing messages back and forth. Also, you don't need to worry about correctly interpreting confusing nonverbal messages such as facial expressions and tone of voice. But that is all hindsight – at that time we were unaware of Asperger Syndrome.

Brent continued to date this woman for several weeks and invited her to our house the next time he came home from college. She sat on the couch in our family room smiling, holding his hand, and putting her arm around him. She continually looked at him with what appeared to be love-struck eyes and was very attentive to him, almost hanging on his every word. In reality, she seemed to do most of the talking.

The next month Brent said she no longer wanted to see him because of a comment he made about her drinking. She had told him about an incident at a party that had occurred before she met him, when she had been drinking heavily and was molested by one of the men at the gathering. Brent responded matter-of-factly that maybe she should not drink so much because then no one would be able to take advantage of her. She became irate, responding that no one was going to ever tell her how much to drink and that she did not think she wanted to see him again. Brent later called her on the phone to try to talk through the situation. He calmly concluded that maybe it was best that they did not continue to go out because she must have a drinking problem considering how she reacted to his reasoned, logical comment. He seemed to take the relationship breakup in stride and continued to chat with other young women via the Internet.

Only a short time later Brent told his dad that he met a woman on the Internet from Arkansas, who was two years older than he was. She had asked Brent if they could "go steady," to which he had agreed. Yet Brent had not met her. In fact, he did not even know what she looked like because she would not send a picture. Press was concerned about Brent's naïvete and tried to explain to him that there were many lonely individuals looking for relationships who might say just about anything to get a date. In addition, he told Brent that there were perpetrators and individuals who just make up identities and even fake being female over the Internet when they are actually male. Brent thought that Press was being ridiculous and insisted that none of this applied to him because he had spoken to this woman on the phone several times and knew she was honest. He also defended his relationship with her by saying that they had many similar interests. Exasperated, Press asked for some examples.

Brent responded that they both liked the color blue! Press was now beside himself. He told Brent that it was impossible to have a relationship and go steady with someone he had never met and that it took more than a mutual liking of a color to establish a relationship.

The clincher came when Brent said that he was going to meet his new friend soon. She had asked him if she could come to Missouri with her two girlfriends and meet at a motel near our home. The girlfriends were supposedly going to sightsee while she and Brent got to know each other. Trying to explain to Brent why this was not a good idea was not easy. Again, he thought we were being ridiculous and overprotective. We pointed out the awkwardness and the significant difficulties and problems associated with being in such an intimate situation, especially for the first meeting. Brent insisted that this was not a sexual meeting, so there was no need to worry. They had specifically discussed that there would be no sexual involvement during this meeting. I suggested that they might not like each other and therefore should meet under less confining and awkward conditions. I even offered that she was welcome to stay at our house for the weekend. Brent said that he would ask her. Press also reminded him that although physical attributes were not necessarily the main criteria people use to decide whether or not to meet someone, they were important and that Brent should consider it a red flag that she had never sent him a picture, even though he had asked for one and had sent her one of him. Brent said that he would think about it and perhaps ask her again for a picture. In the meantime, he asked her about coming to our home rather than a motel, but she was not sure that was a good idea.

Brent finally revealed that the young woman had confided in him about having some physical problems and that she hesitated sending her picture because she had been rejected in the past and did not want to be hurt again. I could not imagine Brent being unkind to her, even if she was physically unattractive. In high school, he volunteered to role play the marriage partner of a very obese girl when no one else in the class was willing to. He was not attracted to her but said that he felt bad for her because no one else wanted to be her partner. They worked together on the class assignment, which included planning a pretend wedding ceremony, budget, and so on. He took the assignment very seriously and completed all the required tasks with his partner. Brent invited me to the mock wedding ceremony. Here the teacher pulled me aside to say that she was proud of Brent because he demonstrated kindness in volunteering to work with his partner, especially when he had no interest in dating her.

The picture of Brent's "steady girlfriend" from Arkansas arrived in the mail at Brent's college dorm shortly after he asked her again to send it. He later told us that he was so shocked by the picture that he could not bring himself to schedule a meeting with her. When asked on the phone to be honest about what he thought when he saw her picture, he responded honestly that he could not envision himself dating her. She was very hurt by his honest answer. He told us her picture was so revolting that he tore it up. Her girlfriends then sent him hate mail telling him how cruel he was to their friend.

Based on the earlier experience, Press and I were shocked that he had answered so bluntly. We thought that he probably should have evaded her question or told a white lie. But Brent insisted that he was being honest because he knew it was wrong to lie. Now we know that individuals with Asperger Syndrome tend to take comments literally and respond to exactly what people ask, not out of meanness but because of their literal interpretation of the request. However, at that time we were very baffled as to why Brent would act in a manner that appeared to be hurtful. He truly seemed confused by our response because he thought that it was best to be honest; he did not think that was hurtful. The irony of the situation was that we began our involvement worrying that Brent might be a victim in this situation and ended up feeling sorry for this young woman, wishing we could protect her from being the victim of our son's hurtful comments.

The next month Brent brought his roommate home from college over the Thanksgiving weekend. We were traveling to Chicago to share Thanksgiving dinner with Press' family, and took Al with us. Brent and Al seemed to get along fairly well despite their age and cultural differences. We asked them how school was going and if they were able to study with the distraction of the computer in the dorm room. Al answered that he did not need to study much because he was taking language classes, which was his area of strength. Brent, on the other hand, indicated that he was not studying much and that he needed to do more. We asked Al if he could encourage Brent to study, assuming that Al was almost like a mentor to Brent.

In looking back on this time, I realize that perhaps Brent and Al were more evenly paired than we had first assumed. They both struggled with the English language. Al was trying to learn as much as possible about American culture and our language. Brent was able to help him, and yet he too had some vague and not well-defined communication issues. But Al seemed to adapt to American culture rather quickly.

A couple of weeks later Brent called to tell us that he had missed one of his final exams because the room had been changed. He had failed to notice that the schedule and room assignments during finals week were different than during the regular semester. We advised him to set his alarm so he could get up early the next morning and go to the professor's office as soon as possible to explain his mistake and ask if it would still be possible to take the exam. We warned him that the professor might say no because he was not required to allow students to make up exams. Luckily, the professor did not penalize Brent for missing the exam and allowed him to take it that day.

Brent attained a C+ average during his first semester; however, the second semester proved to be more academically challenging. We encouraged Brent to initiate appointments with his college advisor to find out what services were available to assist him with his studies and help him make and maintain a study plan. He complied with our request and saw his advisor several times. Press also called the advisor, after Brent gave him permission to do so, to find out what support services were available on campus. We had hoped that there would be a study skills class or a mentoring program that could help support Brent. The advisor suggested that we talk to somebody at the department that assisted students who had a documented disability.

That was when we found out that Brent might have been able to receive services through Vocational Rehabilitation (VR) if he still had carried a special education label. However, he did so well academically in high school that he did not need any special education supports or services, partly because it was a much more structured environment. VR offered mentoring and study programs as well as tuition assistance to qualified university students.

While Brent had not yet received an Asperger Syndrome diagnosis, we found out that students with attention deficit hyperactivity disorder (ADHD) could request academic accommodations with documentation from their physician stating that such strategies were needed in order for them to be successful in the classroom. Dr. Rubin, Brent's psychiatrist, wrote a letter stating that Brent needed untimed tests in small-group settings with minimal distractions.

Up until this time, Brent had not wanted to be singled out as being different and did not want his professors to know that he had ADHD. However, during the second semester Brent was attaining a passing "C" grade in Composition 112, but would not receive a passing grade for the course until he passed the university composition assessment test, which he had already failed twice. This timed test was administered in a large group. We encouraged Brent to request accommodations so he might have a better testing environment, especially since this was his last chance to pass. Brent agreed and requested the accommodations Dr. Rubin suggested. Although he took the test in a quiet room without the usual time constraints, he failed. This meant that he needed to repeat the entire course. I spoke several times with the English professor, who did not realize that Brent had any learning difficulties. However, he did notice that Brent seemed to have some difficulty organizing his ideas into a coherent and cohesive composition during Composition 112. Several years later Brent told us that he did not study for the test, so the accommodations were probably irrelevant.

Brent called us just prior to spring break to tell us that he wanted to stay at the university because he was tired of driving the 95-mile trip home. He had nothing to do at home or at school, so he preferred to stay on campus. He indicated that the dorm was open because the international students needed to have a place to stay over the short break. We agreed to his request, but asked if he would come home for a few days toward the end of the break, so we could visit with him. When he called several days later, we found out that he had failed to notice the signs posted all over campus indicating that students wanting to remain on campus over the break needed to contact the housing office ahead of time in order to rent a room in the only dorm building that was going to be open over the vacation. On the first evening of the break Brent stayed in his dorm room watching television by himself. He said that he thought the dorm was very quiet, but did not realize until the next day that he was the only one staying there. The housing office was closed, but he talked to several Internet buddies one of whom offered him a place to stay until he could contact the housing office to rent a dorm room. Although Brent had missed the posted signs and had not planned any activities over the break, we complimented him on his resourcefulness in finding a place to stay and suggested that he offer to pay for a meal or offer some compensation for being able to stay over at his friend's off-campus apartment.

Toward the end of the second semester Brent allowed us to help him draft a letter to the university requesting academic assistance during his sophomore year to help compensate for his weaknesses in auditory processing, attention, concentration, and planning and organizational skills. We sent along all of Brent's previous educational diagnostic reports, as well as the letter from his psychiatrist requesting untimed tests in a small, quiet group setting. Again, Brent complied with our requests to go to the office on campus that provided academic assistance. I spoke to the director of the program several times and asked for clarification on their services. I was basically told that the student needed to be motivated to ask for assistance and that Brent had to be able to describe what type of assistance he needed.

The problem was that Brent did not know! It is typically very difficult for individuals with Asperger Syndrome to ask for help and communicate their needs. I explained that I did not expect someone from the school program to knock on Brent's door each morning and pull him out of bed to attend classes and tutoring sessions. However, it would be helpful if someone could mentor him or initiate calling him to see how things were going, given that Brent had difficulty initiating such contacts and communicating his needs. No such program existed for Brent.

Brent continued to chat on the Internet and met several young women from across the United States that way. They exchanged pictures and letters, and some of these contacts continued throughout the summer break after he came home from college. He told me that he had been on many dates, but frequently he only went out once with each girl. He later described these as "hi, good-bye dates." Sometimes, young women from the university would e-mail and ask him to meet them by the school tower. He would go to the designated place, but was sometimes stood up.

After one of these disappointments, I said to Brent, "I wonder if it is difficult for you to talk in person to young women, at least more difficult than it is to write and chat on the computer." Looking absolutely shocked, he asked how I knew that. I did not want to insult him, but I thought how obvious that seemed given his track record. I imagined that the young women expected him to be able to converse as well verbally as he did in writing.

Sophomore Year

After rooming with Al for a year, Brent suddenly decided that he needed to switch roommates. He did not approve of Al's behavior with young women. Moreover, he believed that Al's interest in the women was strictly sexual, which Brent emphatically denounced as wrong and inappropriate behavior. I remember being surprised that Brent took such a strong stand on this issue. However, we were pleased that when he took a stand on an important issue, he usually maintained it firmly. He also stated that he and Al did not seem to have anything in common anymore. Except for watching an occasional movie together, they did not share common interests. Finally, Brent felt that Al was taking advantage of him by frequently asking to borrow his car. Brent seemed to have difficulty telling him that this made him uncomfortable. Reportedly, Al was surprised when Brent abruptly moved out of the dorm room. I imagine the issues between them were not discussed, partly because Brent assumed that Al should know how he felt.

Shortly after Brent settled into his new dorm room, his new roommate moved out to share a room with one of his friends. Brent was alone for one week and said he liked the privacy. After all, he did not have to share the computer terminal with anyone else! Another student in the dorm told Brent that the housing office would charge him more money to keep a private room if he did not get a new roommate soon. This young man was also living alone and offered to be Brent's roommate. Brent did not know much about this student when he agreed to move in with him. He later described him as very quiet. Reportedly, they did not have much in common either and did not share meals or participate in activities together. Brent began staying on campus on the weekends more frequently, while his roommate left campus most weekends. Again, this allowed unlimited access to the computer. It seemed as though Brent and his roommate tolerated each other, but did not talk much together. The roommate invited his own friends over to their dorm room several times late at night without asking Brent's permission. Brent found this annoying because he could not get to sleep when they were in the room. He continued to eat his meals in the cafeteria with Al's friends and later in the semester with students on campus whom he met over the Internet.

During the first semester of sophomore year, Brent maintained a C+ average without any academic assistance. Just prior to his second semester, we encouraged him to retake an introduction to using the computer class he had taken during his freshman year because he had attained a "D." If there was one class Brent could ace, it should have been computers – he spent most of his time on the computer chatting and learning how to operate it and write programs. But he could not make himself read the textbook because he found it to be boring and a waste of time. Apparently, the teacher had also commented that Brent always looked tired and seemed to have an attitude problem that suggested that he did not want to be in class. Although Brent had never experimented with illegal drugs, we tried to tell him that the teacher might have suspected that drugs were one of the reasons he displayed an "I don't care attitude." Brent thought this was ridiculous. He never tried drugs, and just assumed that the teacher would know that. Again, this seemed to be reflective of a theory-of-mind issue. That is, Brent had not entertained the idea that his teacher could have an entirely different perspective than his. Brent got a different teacher when he repeated the computer course, and he attained an "A" average.

Classes became increasingly more difficult for Brent during the second semester. By the middle of the semester, he virtually quit going to classes without telling us. He finally told us that he needed to make up work in science and promised to talk to the teacher about getting help. Later he admitted that he was so far behind in science that there was no hope of catching up. His weight lifting teacher promised that if he came to the remaining classes, he would pass. But Brent later told us that he frequently could not attend the class because his erratic sleeping patterns were making it difficult for him to wake up on time.

We were trying to be supportive from a distance because we wanted Brent to be as independent as possible, and yet we did not want to set him up for failure by offering no assistance and totally removing ourselves from his life. We were confused about how to best help him, so we continued to call him and ask how he was doing. I remember trying to make suggestions in a way that would not appear too intrusive. For example, I told him that teachers usually liked when students went to them with questions or to ask for help because it showed that they were interested and trying to be successful. Brent was not telling us much about school at this time, probably because he was overwhelmed. In looking back, he must have felt as though he was drowning and had no options except to avoid school by staying up late at night on the Internet and sleeping late in the morning, often missing classes.

Just prior to summer break, Brent announced that he did not like the university because the work was too hard and he did not want to return in the fall. We suggested that perhaps he should take some time off to figure out what he wanted to do next. In the meantime, he moved home and started working at McDonald's. Brent did not realize it but around this time the university was preparing to send him a letter stating that he was on academic probation because of poor grades and would not be able to return to school in the fall.

Meanwhile, two weeks after Brent moved back home, Kristen graduated high school with honors one year earlier than originally anticipated. She was agonizing over what college to attend and whether she should live at home or on a college campus. She wanted to live at home and commute to school because her boyfriend lived in our town. However, they broke up soon afterwards, and she decided in July to live away at an academically challenging state university. Kristen seemed to immensely enjoy the two years she lived with us while her brother was away at college. It was the first time in her life that she was able to feel like an only child and did not have to take a back seat to Brent. Now he was back home and she was moving out!

The Second College Experience

Because of Brent's intense interest in computers, Press and I suggested that he consider attending a more hands-on program that specifically taught computer skills. He agreed and we went to an open house at DeVry Institute to find out more about their programs. DeVry is designed for commuting students, offering two- and four-year technical programs leading to associate and bachelor degrees. The school was located 30 miles from our home. Brent thought that DeVry's program was better designed to meet his needs than the university program. Most of the courses were taught hands-on in the laboratory, and significantly fewer liberal art courses were required. Further, many of the liberal arts courses Brent had already taken would transfer. This meant that he could start taking computer courses immediately and would have a lighter class schedule than most of the other students. We all thought that a lighter schedule would be beneficial and would help Brent to be more successful and confident.

Brent selected the four-year computer programming track of study and began taking classes in July of 1996, just less than two months after he left the university. DeVry's structured program would only take him about three years to complete because classes also met in the summer for a full year of study. Full-time students met for all of their classes either in the morning or in the afternoon, allowing them the rest of the day to work and earn money. Most of the students were several years older than the average college freshman, and they needed to work to support themselves or their families. Brent continued to work part-time at McDonald's until he was offered a part-time computer programming position at a small Christian company the following March.

After doing well academically during the first semester at DeVry, Brent decided to change his major to telecommunications. Fortunately, he did not lose any of the credits because all of DeVry's programs had the same requirements for the first semester. Although Brent seemed somewhat less motivated during the second semester, he did fairly well.

Brent did not date during this time and generally had a very limited social life. We suggested that he join some clubs at DeVry and visit with some of the students from his classes during their free time. He did join one club for a short period. In addition, one of the students occasionally called him, but Brent thought he was odd and did not want to continue the relationship. I did not want to interfere in Brent's life and orchestrate his social world as I had tried to do when he was younger. However, he seemed to need some coaching or modeling to initiate social relationships.

By the third semester at DeVry, Brent's grades started to decline, and he began skipping classes. We did not know that he was skipping because he was taking afternoon classes, and we were at work when he was supposed to be leaving for school. When I found him napping as I arrived home from work several times, he explained that class got out early. This seemed believable until it began occurring on a regular basis. Then we realized that he was regularly skipping school and falling behind again.

That May he was hospitalized for a suicide attempt. While he was in the hospital, he asked us to withdraw him from DeVry. Although he has never been able to fully articulate how he was feeling, it seems likely that he was overwhelmed with school and the social difficulties he was experiencing, combined with an inability to communicate that and problem solve his predicament. After Brent returned from the hospital, he took two weeks off from his computer job. When he returned to work, he requested more hours and was virtually working full-time, with some flexibility in his schedule, until he was fired in March of 1998.

Relationships

A week or so before Brent lost his job, he joined Press and me one day while we shopped for family room furniture. This was unusual because Brent never wanted to shop with us, and as a result we had stopped asking him to join us. Who could blame him? What 21-year-old wants to shop with his parents? Press had planned to go to the computer store after we spent 45 minutes to an hour at a local furniture store, and that seemed to entice Brent to join us and get out of the house.

A young saleswoman in the furniture store recognized Brent from the university and started talking to him. Lisa had recently graduated with a degree in interior design, and this was her first job. She was bubbly and friendly and seemed interested in Brent. When she left us to take care of another customer, Brent admitted that he liked her and would like to ask her for a date. Press offered several suggestions on how to start up a conversation and see if she was free to date. When Lisa came back to assist us, Brent talked to her, but mostly answered her questions. She was very personable and outgoing and told Brent that she needed to move back into her parents' home for the time being until she could save enough money to move out on her own. When she heard that we were buying family room furniture so Brent could have the old furniture for the basement apartment Press had built for him, Lisa said that she was envious. Brent smiled and continued to talk with her. We stayed at the store for several hours looking for furniture, which did not upset Brent in the least! Each time Lisa left to speak with her boss, Brent asked for more suggestions on how to converse with her.

When we finally left the store we had purchased a complete set of family room furniture, but Brent still had not asked for Lisa's phone number. We tried to make the situation easier for him by walking away several times so he could speak alone with her. After we left the store, Brent told us that he really wanted to ask for her telephone number and see if she was free to date, but he just could not get up the nerve. Press suggested that Brent call the store a few days later and ask to speak with Lisa. He could then find out if she would like to exchange home phone numbers. Moreover, she had said that she would be calling us to see if we had any questions regarding the sale; hopefully Brent could answer the phone when she called.

Brent did call her several days later, and she immediately indicated that she would like to go out. She suggested that they go dancing the following Friday night. Brent had not danced in years and was not sure where young adults went to dance, so he got on the computer to find out. After talking on the phone several times during the week, they met as planned. Brent told us that she ordered an alcoholic drink, and he asked if he could taste it because he did not have much experience ordering drinks. Brent came home very happy. They had had a wonderful time and were going to see each other again.

Lisa and Brent continued to date on her days off for several weeks. In addition, they talked on the phone several times each week. I have no idea what they talked about, but I could hear Brent frequently laughing from several rooms away. One time Lisa asked him if he would surprise her and pick out an activity for them to do on their next date. Brent decided to take her to the zoo and gave her a red rose when he picked her up, which she found very sweet. Shortly after that Lisa told Brent that she was going to look at model homes on her next day off with one of her girlfriends; she would call him about getting together. Brent called her several times that day to see when they were getting together. When she finally answered the phone in the evening, he persistently questioned what she had been doing all day and why she had not called him. Lisa said that she wanted to treat Brent to a date since he had paid for all their previous dates. After he picked her up, she explained that she had had difficulty with men in the past and was in counseling to work through these issues. Therefore, she thought it was best that they did not continue to date. She was very nice to Brent and told him that he was a great person and that she had a good time with him, but she just was not ready for a serious relationship. Brent was disappointed, but he seemed to be able to move on and not dwell on the loss.

He continued to chat with women on the Internet; in addition, when we received our phone bill we found out that he had contacted dating services. We were shocked at the cost of the two-minute phone calls that Brent made to follow up on dating leads. We made Brent pay for his portion of the phone bill, and he promised not to make any more of these expensive calls. He had no idea that the supposedly free dating service would cost so much. Press explained that it was impossible for the dating service to stay in business if their services were really free, as Brent claimed they advertised. They were making a profit off the phone calls. A good dating match did not materialize.

Press and I became concerned that Brent seemed to be overly focused on finding a girlfriend. He told us that he thought he was the only sexually inexperienced 22-year-old man in the world. He probably was in the minority, but certainly not the only one. We tried to explain to him that this was not bad, even though society would make it seem so. I attempted to clarify that relationships with women did not have to involve sex and that it would be best to focus his efforts on establishing a friendship with a young woman, rather than on a physical relationship. I also pointed out that he could meet single women at work, school, and church and that he could get to know them in person rather than communicating on the Internet sight unseen, never knowing for sure if they were telling the truth. We had already told him several times that for safety reasons he was never to meet women from the Internet whom he did not know at their homes but rather in a public place. Brent thought that he was immune from this and that we were being ridiculous and overprotective.

Brent continued to chat on the Internet and occasionally received phone calls from young women. One cold and icy winter afternoon he told us that he was going to meet a young woman, Mindy, at the shopping mall near our house. An hour later he called to tell us that he had been in an accident and was not sure if his car was drivable. He had slid on the ice; luckily, he was not hurt and no one else was involved in the accident. Press agreed to meet him and determine if his car was drivable or needed to be towed. That was when we found out that he was in Kansas and had lied to us about meeting Mindy at the mall. He admitted that he was on his way to her apartment. He had already met her once before unbeknown to us and was going to meet her for a secret rendezvous. As providence would have it, he never arrived at her apartment. I agreed to call and let her know that he had been in an accident.

The next day Brent, Press, and I left for a seven-day cruise ship vacation. During the trip Press had several heart-to-heart talks with Brent about relationships. Following these conversations, Brent told Press that he was fortunate that the car accident prevented him from going to Mindy's house because he was focused on sex and was going to meet her for the wrong reasons. He then told his dad that he wanted to wait for a physical relationship until he married.

Mindy continued to call Brent when we returned from vacation. Once she even drove to our house to meet Brent because his car was still in the auto body shop for repairs after the accident. I think Mindy felt very uncomfortable meeting us. Although she seemed to be trying to get her life back on track, she was culturally, emotionally, and socially very different from Brent.

Brent decided that he did not want to continue talking with Mindy, but he did not know how to tell her. When she called one evening, he told her that he was busy, and went to watch television without hanging the phone up. When Press came downstairs later to use the phone and found out what happened, he explained to Brent why it was not appropriate to keep Mindy hanging and pointed out that he needed to explain his feelings to her. Mindy called back and asked to talk to Press because she heard the conversation between Press and Brent. Press was embarrassed because he did not realize that she overheard him talking to Brent prior to hanging up the phone. Brent pleaded with Press to explain to Mindy that he did not want to continue the relationship. Press did speak to her briefly and with Brent's permission explained that he had Asperger Syndrome, which affected him socially. Mindy responded by saying that she knew something was different about Brent. He was unlike anyone else she had ever met, but she truly liked him. She found him "refreshing." Most of the men she had been involved with before were abusive and took advantage of her. I imagine that she was attracted to Brent because of his good looks and kind spirit. He was not manipulative and abusive, but innocent and naïve.

While chatting on the Internet several weeks later, Brent encountered Marissa, the young bubbly woman who spent a lot of time with Brent's first college roommate. Although Brent had emphatically stated that he did not approve of her relationship with his ex-roommate several years earlier, he was now very interested in meeting her and getting reacquainted. They began dating, and Brent quickly fell head over heels for her. She had not been married before, and they talked about getting married within the year. He was convinced that he had found his future wife. He remarked that he wanted to get married soon and that it did not make sense that his younger sister was already married before he was. This was an example of how Brent felt that Kristen was getting ahead of him even though she was younger.

Although Marissa was only two years older than Brent, she had done a lot of living in those years, including having a child.

She came to our home for dinner with her adorable young daughter several times, and Brent invited his friends over to his basement apartment several times to meet her. His closest friend from church later shared that he did not think this was the relationship God had intended for him. Soon after that Marissa and Brent broke up, and Brent impulsively blurted out to us that she was too obsessed with sex and was glad the relationship was over!

The Third College Experience

During the fall of 1999, Brent decided to attend school again to obtain hands-on instruction in computer technology. He interviewed at two college programs and decided to attend Vatterott College because of the structure of their program. He especially liked the fact that Vatterott only offered one course at a time. Each course met from 6 p.m. to 10 p.m. Monday through Thursday for 10 weeks. Most of the course was conducted in the computer lab with plenty of time for hands-on practice of the skills taught. Furthermore, no liberal arts courses were involved. The other program that he considered met twice a week, required a considerable amount of homework outside of class, and involved some liberal arts courses. Although the latter program offered a degree, Brent decided that he would most likely be more successful with Vatterott's structured program.

Brent was absolutely correct. He completed Vatterott College 60 weeks later achieving a 90 percent overall grade point average. However, these 60 weeks did not proceed smoothly all of the time. After the first couple of days at Vatterott Brent seemed content. Nonetheless, right after he appeared to have settled into the new routine, he insisted that he was not going to continue because he believed the program had been misrepresented to him. He stayed home that evening. It was difficult to process what was causing Brent to be so upset. Several hours later, he stated that he was told that there was NO homework at Vatterott, and yet his teacher had told the class that there would be a little homework. This made

Brent very agitated. He thought NO homework meant absolutely NO homework! We were able to clarify these concerns with his teacher the next day and share with Brent the fact that only a minimal amount of homework would be required. This seemed to satisfy him and he attended school again after missing one evening class.

Individuals with Asperger Syndrome tend to take people at their word and expect things to happen exactly as stated. I imagine this is what caused Brent so much distress. However, Press and I were surprised to see Brent digging his heels in on this issue. Even though transitions and change are very difficult for individuals with Asperger Syndrome, we had not seen Brent experience as much difficulty with change before. Even when we moved twice during his junior high and high school years, he handled these changes better than most adolescents would.

After the homework incident Brent seemed to get along with his teacher and was academically successful throughout the rest of the 10-week term. But during the beginning of the second 10-week term Brent became upset again, this time deciding that he did not want to continue with school because of a "stupid rule" his teacher decided to enforce. He stayed home from school and sent an angry e-mail to his teacher telling him how disgusted he was that the teacher now required compliance with the school rule of prohibiting snacks in the computer lab.

Our first reaction was to make sure Brent understood the reason for the rule. He had been in many computer classes and never had a problem complying with the rule because he knew that it was necessary so that no food or drink would be spilled on the computers. He said that he knew the reason behind the rule, but that it was not fair that the other computer teacher was not enforcing it. Furthermore, he said that he was hungry and thirsty, and that his teacher had not enforced the rule during the last term! Brent had the same teacher for his first three terms. He later disclosed that the teacher gave them a break every hour and that he was able to get snacks and eat and drink them in the hall at those times. So his concern about being hungry and thirsty was not the issue. He seemed to be stuck on his definition of fairness.

I tried to reflect Brent's feelings back to him rather than debate the sensibility of the rule. I responded to his exasperation by saying that whatever was bothering him about this situation must be very important to him, given that he was willing to quit school and a possible future career in computers for his beliefs. He said it was very important to him, and he seemed relieved that I understood his passion. Actually I did not understand his reasoning at all. However, I did sense his passion regarding the issue.

Normally, Press and/or I attempt to process meltdown situations with Brent soon after they occur. However, this time we decided to follow Dr. McCartney's advice and waited a few days. Interestingly enough, Brent told me several times over the next few days that he was ready to process the situation and asked when we were planning to do so. We replied that we might be available in a few days. We did not feel rushed since school was closed for a couple of days, so he would not be missing any classes.

Brent shared his dilemma with his social skills counselor, Matt, when they had their weekly meeting, as discussed in more detail in Chapter Ten. Apparently, Matt suggested that Brent make a list of the pros and cons of the situation before making a decision. Press and I had suggested this strategy many times in the past to no avail – but after all we were just his parents! What did we know? When Matt suggested it, it was a revelation Brent had not considered. As a result, the day before school reopened Brent told us that the pros of attending school far outweighed the cons and that he had decided to continue to attend school.

But the incident was not completely over, because the teacher had forwarded Brent's angry e-mail to the admissions counselor. The admissions counselor was very upset by Brent's tone and told me that she was shocked because she had never observed this side of him. Brent did not make any threats to the teacher or the school, but it was obvious from the words in the e-mail that he was very agitated.

We decided to meet with the teacher and counselor to discuss the situation and also explain Asperger Syndrome if necessary. Brent's teacher was very positive about having Brent in his class and shared that he thought everyone was making more of the situation than was warranted. At that point the counselor noted that she had been shocked and was concerned about Brent's reaction. The teacher indicated that he wanted Brent back in class right away so he could get reacclimated. Brent agreed and attended the next class session. Brent's teacher truly liked him and was willing to make accommodations if necessary to help Brent be successful. Although Brent experienced some difficulties when he switched teachers, we did not ask to meet with the school team again, because we wanted Brent to learn to take care of these glitches in a more independent manner.

By the next spring Brent met a young woman over the Internet whom he wanted to visit. Press and I were overseas on vacation for two weeks at the time, and Brent was at home by himself. Before we left, he had promised he would not drive to meet any new person that he might encounter on the Internet until we were back home. Almost immediately after he met us at the airport upon our return, he announced that he had met a young woman, Melinda, over the Internet, and that he wanted permission to visit her for the first time the upcoming weekend. Several weeks later we found out that he had driven two hours to her college to visit her while we were gone. However, at least he obeyed our safety rule and told Matt where he was going and left him the telephone number where he could be reached. He also called Matt when he returned to say that he had arrived home safely.

Several weeks later when the spring semester was over, Melinda returned to her father's home, which was approximately four and one half hours from our home, because she had failed most of her courses and could not return to college for summer school. Melinda did not have a driver's license, so she took the train to visit Brent and us over Memorial Day. She stayed at our home for two days and left a note thanking us for our hospitality. She wrote that we had done a good job raising Brent because he was such a caring and kind person. Brent spent most of the rest of the summer driving up to see her when he was not in school. She also came back with him several times and stayed in town for the next weekend. To pass time she went to Vatterott with him, remaining in the school lobby reading or drawing while he was in class.

Melinda seemed to really like Brent and appeared to be a good influence on him. They seemed to complement each other. While she was at our home, she insisted that he study for his exams and helped him study. But we soon observed that she acted like an overprotective mother, making suggestions on Brent's diet, daily habits, and so on. Brent did not seem to mind, as he was very fond of her. They looked happy together and spent hours watching movies and going to the arcades over the summer. When they were at her house Melinda cooked him breakfast and enjoyed caring for him. She proudly announced that she believed that her weaknesses were his strengths and his weaknesses were her strengths, which she thought made them very compatible. One afternoon when I was proofreading one of my graduate students' papers, I asked Melinda a question about the use of commas. She wanted to write children's books and was very knowledgeable about writing conventions. Brent interrupted and said, "Do you want to know how I decide if a comma belongs in a sentence? I just look at the sentence and see if it looks good there, then I add it. I don't know the comma rules." He then started laughing. Melinda chimed in that they each possessed different areas of knowledge and that was another way they complemented each other.

Melinda continued to tell us that when the summer was over she was going to look for a job and learn how to drive. She was afraid to drive because two of her father's cousins had been killed in a car accident when they were teenagers. Reportedly, her father was pushing her to get a driver's license because they lived in a rural area, which made it necessary to drive in order to be able to get to work. As the end of the summer approached, I asked about her plans. She became very upset and told Brent that we were materialistic. This seemed like an overreaction to my question. As a reaction to her father's pushing her to look for a job, she must have misinterpreted the intention of my question as an attack or demand.

Around this time Brent realized one day that he had very little money left in his checking account. He and Melinda had spent most of his money at the arcades during the past few weeks, and he had not been keeping track of how much he had spent until we asked him to balance his checkbook. When he called to tell her that he would not be able to see her over the upcoming weekend and might need to visit her every other weekend, because he did not have enough money for gasoline, she became enraged and told him that she believed the real reason for his not coming was that his parents did not want him to continue seeing her. As she displayed more and more of this behavior, Brent thought that maybe they shouldn't see each other so much and told her so.

Brent felt sorry for Melinda because of her family situation. She wanted to move out of her dad's home and by the next year hoped to be able to move near our home. Concerned that she might want a baby in order to get married and leave her home, I asked him if she seemed to focus on babies, especially since her 18-year-old sister and husband were having a baby. I explained that some young women get pregnant either consciously or unconsciously to leave home. Brent responded, "No, she is not that kind of girl." Yet a couple of minutes later he admitted that she had been doing something that bothered him. Every time he spent the weekend at her house, they went to Wal-Mart because, except for a small movie theater, there was nothing else to do for entertainment near her home. As soon as they walked into the store, she would run over to look at the baby department and ooh and ah at how cute the baby clothes and other items were.

Brent and Melinda did break up at the end of the summer, but only after Melinda tried several tactics to get Brent back. For example, she contacted a woman he had met on the Internet and shared some of the games and tricks she used to talk him into dating her again. Several weeks after Brent started to date this woman, she in turn shared Melinda's strategy with him, confirming what we had suspected all along. For example, either Melinda or a friend of hers contacted Brent via the Internet claiming to be a shaman (fortuneteller) who was led to contact him. This supposed shaman continued to steer the Internet conversation back to his ex-girlfriend, trying to convince him that he truly loved her. By the end of the two-and-a-half-hour conversation, Brent was sure that he truly loved her and needed to call her.

Melinda acted surprised when he called that night professing his love. When Brent told us that he planned to go to her home the next day for a four-day weekend, we pointed out that although we could not stop him, we believed that he was acting impulsively and asked him to think it over one more day. If he still wanted to see her, he would still have three days to visit. We reminded him that he had acted impulsively several times in the past and had been sorry about his behavior afterwards. Press also told Brent that the fortunetelling conversation via the Internet was a scam and suggested that he talk to his minister about it. By this time it was close to midnight and Brent agreed to wait to call Melinda until the next day.

The response he received about fortunetelling from his minister combined with Melinda's angry reaction to his call that he would not be coming to her house that day made him decide that he did not want to continue seeing her. Although he never saw her again, she was not completely out of his life because she soon started e-mailing him that she was very nauseous and losing weight. A week later she dropped the bomb! Supposedly, he was going to be a father. She would only allow him to see his child if he relocated in the town next to hers. After several weeks of anguish on all sides, she announced that she was not pregnant after all!

Lessons Learned

Brent did not leave home after college to lead an independent life. It was during these years that we found out that he had Asperger Syndrome, a lifelong disability. Independence may take longer for Brent. Press and I constantly try to evaluate how much support and assistance to give him because we do not want to foster dependence. We would like to put the proper supports in place so he can experience the positive situations and success necessary to foster self-confidence and the desire and ability to be independent.

Brent told his psychiatrist that the most discouraging aspects of Asperger Syndrome are the impulsivity and the addictive-type behavior he experiences. As we have just seen, Brent began to focus his attention on obtaining a serious girlfriend, pursuing this perseverative and all-consuming interest with the same intensity he applied to earlier interests. Despite discussions with his psychologist, and advice of church friends, his social skills counselor, and us, Brent still seemed to need to obsess on dating and chasing this all-consuming interest. Fortunately, to date, there have been no life-changing problems associated with these life lessons. Following his courtship with Melinda, Brent seemed to work on developing relationships, rather than searching for physical unions. For example, he attended church activities where he could meet young adults in safe group situations. However, a new chapter seems to be developing as I write these words. Brent's obsession with dating has resurfaced. Again, Press and I are concerned about his ability to make appropriate decisions regarding these relationships.

chapter seven

The World
of Adult Work

Adult work experiences for Brent proved to be filled with mine fields and were fraught with many challenges, as were dating and college experiences. When Brent came home from college during his freshman spring break, he stated that he no longer wanted to spend the summer college break working as a sacker at the local supermarket, as he had done during high school. In looking for other opportunities, we noticed an advertisement in the newspaper for a job fair sponsored by an amusement park located 12 miles from our home. Press and Kristen, then 16 years old, accompanied Brent to the shopping mall where the job fair was being held. Brent was immediately offered a job in the maintenance department. Kristen, on the other hand, was upset because it took her several interviews that day to land a job in one of the restaurants at the park. After accepting their jobs, they received information on when to report for orientation and where to purchase their uniforms.

Brent came home the weekend of his scheduled orientation, and after we had given him directions, he set out for the amusement park. About 45 minutes later, he called us from a gas station. He was lost, had driven well over 20 miles, even though the park was only 12 miles away, and was already late for the orientation. Apparently, he missed the turn onto the major highway and had continued for over 10 miles past the exit for the amusement park.

Furthermore, his gas tank was registering empty, and he did not know what to do. Press reminded him that he had just told us he was calling from a pay phone located on the property of a gas station and that he should stop there to fill his car with gas before coming back home. We also agreed to call the amusement park and explain that he had gotten lost and needed to reschedule his orientation for another weekend. Fortunately, there were still several other orientation sessions available for college students.

We learned from this experience that we needed to tell Brent what landmarks he would see if he drove too far or missed his turn so he could look for them and realize that he had made a mistake before he had traveled too far. We also realized that in the future Brent probably needed to drive to a location where he had never been before with a passenger who could provide directions before he attempted to drive there on his own. When Brent was a passenger, he did not seem to be as adept at finding new places the next time he drove on his own as he was when he did the actual driving. Brent also began leaving the house a little earlier to allow extra time in case he got lost. Using these strategies, he successfully found the amusement park on his own and attended the next orientation.

Brent performed routine maintenance tasks and operated some of the amusement rides for a while before he and another young man were asked by the manager if they would like to earn $1 an hour more by cleaning the restrooms. Brent agreed, telling us that in addition to paying more that job kept him out of the hot sun. He did not like working outdoors and tired easily. He was also quick to say that he basically just hosed down the bathrooms and did not have to clean them with his hands. When I asked him during the course of the summer how his day went and if he had lunch with any of the other workers, he would say his day was okay but that he did not want to do this job on a long-term basis. Who could blame him? In fact, Press and I were secretly hoping that getting a college degree would be more enticing to Brent after this work experience. Occasionally he ate lunch with someone, but not often, and he did not talk much to fellow workers. I remember feeling bad because he seemed to be a loner; however, I do not think he felt that bad himself. On the other hand, his sister met her first boyfriend at the park, began dating him and socializing with others, was asked to work extra hours, and was doing some relief management work at the park restaurant. She was hoping to work there the following summer as a manager with her boyfriend. This was in sharp contrast to Brent's more solitary job and general working life.

Adamant about not wanting to work at the amusement park the following summer, Brent came home during spring break in 1996 and applied for a crew position at a McDonald's restaurant located only three miles from our home. Kristen had broken up with her boyfriend and decided not to return to the amusement park since he was still working there. Instead, she had begun working at McDonald's several months before Brent applied. She was not happy about Brent working at the same place because her brother embarrassed her. However, it was tolerable since she and Brent rarely worked the same shift, and did not have the same duties. Kristen was paid a little more per hour because she was given more responsibility to open the store in the early morning and to work directly with the customers. Brent did not feel comfortable working at the cash register, and instead mainly cooked the food and mopped the floors. He resented being asked to mop the floors at night because he was selected to do this duty more than the other crew staff. Occasionally the young men who were the swing shift managers seemed to take advantage of him and were unkind. Kristen said that sometimes they teased Brent and encouraged him to talk about inappropriate topics, such as sex, while he was at work. Brent did not understand why this was inappropriate since the others talked about sex too. He did not realize that they did it in a more subtle manner and knew when not to engage in this type of conversation.

Brent continued to work at McDonald's during the 1996 fall semester while commuting to DeVry. However, as 1997 approached he seemed to find it harder and harder to go to work, although he was not able to put into words what was bothering him. I came home from work several times and found him sleeping in the late afternoon when he was supposed to be getting ready to go to work. I explained to him that it was not acceptable just to stay home and not call work to say that he would not be coming or would be late. He was able to tell me that he did not feel well, but was unable to offer any more explanation about how or what he was feeling. Several times I asked if I could make him something to eat while he showered and told him that I could drive him into work if that would help. He agreed and let me drive him to work twice.

Brent did not work many hours at McDonald's, so we did not think that the job could be stressful for him. However, after hearing Temple Grandin, an adult with high-functioning autism, talk about careers for individuals on the autism spectrum, we now know that working in fast food restaurants is very stressful for persons with Asperger Syndrome because of the demands to work fast, interact with people, operate the cash register, and understand the social nuances associated with dealing with the public. Furthermore, these jobs typically do not pay well and are frequently considered menial. It must have been very frustrating and demeaning for Brent to realize that he could not successfully handle employment that is frequently considered to be lower status.

Mark Romoser, an adult with autism who graduated from Yale, contends that individuals with ASD experience "malemployment" (Romoser, 2000, p. 246), which he defines as not only working below your skill level but also at a task that is completely unsuitable for you. In thinking back, this must have been an exasperating and overwhelming time in Brent's life, given the mismatched work experience combined with his frustration at school and his inability to express his feelings.

We suggested that Brent consider looking for another job if he did not want to stay at McDonald's. He was missing many of the social cues, which led others to tease and take advantage of him. Moreover, he was constantly being asked to work faster, even though he was working as fast as he could. In addition, Brent was more than likely depressed and/or overwhelmed by school and work and unable to put these feelings into words. We now realize that when Brent becomes overwhelmed, he tends to sleep a lot, as he was doing during this time.

During the spring of the same year, Brent found a notice on the church bulletin board advertising for a part-time computer programmer for a local Christian company. He initiated a call to the company to request an interview. The company offered him $6 per hour when he started in April, stating that they were a startup company and that they hoped to raise his salary after becoming firmly established. Since Brent did not have the college credentials to be called a computer programmer and was training while on the job, we all felt that this was a good opportunity and learning experience for him. This job also afforded Brent flexibility in scheduling his work hours around his computer classes. The staff seemed very caring and accepting. We were thrilled that Brent had found such an apparently nurturing and supportive place of employment. Each morning prior to the beginning of the workday, the staff met together to pray. Shortly after he began working part-time, they prayed that Brent would eventually become a full-time employee. He felt accepted and part of the organization and referred to this job opportunity as a computer programmer as his "first real job." He did become a full-time employee in July of 1997 after he withdrew from college for the second time.

We were so pleased that the owner of the company, Greg Danz, seemed to want to take Brent under his wing and allowed Brent flexibility in his work hours when he did not feel that he could work a full eight-hour day. In fact, Brent had only been working part-time a few weeks when he needed to be hospitalized. Press called Greg to ask if Brent could have some time off from work because he was experiencing stress. Greg reassured him that Brent could take all the time he needed and that they would hold his job for him. He never specifically asked Press why Brent needed the time off.

Press was so grateful over this very understanding and nurturing attitude that he stopped at the office one day during his lunch break to meet the staff and thank them. When he arrived, he asked if it was possible to speak to Greg, and was immediately taken to his office. The company had just moved to a new location and was in the process of renovating an entire floor of the building. As Press walked through the makeshift office areas to get to Greg's office, he noticed that although the physical plant was in a state of chaos due to the renovation, the staff were remarkably friendly and appeared to enjoy their work.

Greg warmly introduced himself and humbly noted that although he was the owner of the company, God was actually Chairman of the Board. He further explained to Press that earlier in the year while the company had been working out of a much smaller location near his home, they had been praying for God to reveal another location for their business if it was His will. It was shortly after this time that an associate, Ned, reportedly offered them free office space in this prestigious downtown location. Press asked questions about how the business started, their goals, and Brent's role because Brent had not been able to tell us about the company's overall purpose and operations. Greg also shared that he had been a social worker prior to becoming a businessman and that his wife was a special education teacher. This seemed to cement in Press' mind that Brent was in a work environment that would be very accepting and nurturing of his differences. At that time, we did not know that Brent had Asperger Syndrome; we still believed that he had a learning disability and difficulties with attention that caused him to process information differently.

Several months later, in January of 1998, Brent came home from work one day and shared with us that he had been asked to take a few days off from work and consider whether or not he wanted to return. He was told that this was not a punishment and that he was welcome to return. Furthermore, we were welcome to call Greg or the new president, Max, if we wanted clarification. Since we were very confused, we called Greg and set up an appointment to meet. Greg assured us over the phone that Brent was not being fired and that he thought he just needed some time off because he seemed to be stressed. He was glad that Press had called because he had been noticing that Brent was different and thought we could shed some light on how they could best work with him.

During the meeting, Greg assured us that Brent was a valuable employee and that he would never be fired. Moreover, if the management ever had any concerns about Brent, they would contact us to discuss the situation and come up with a solution together. Max told us that he believed Brent was like a diamond in the rough. I felt as though we were back at those painful special education meetings discussing Brent's challenges during his elementary school years, even though those days were long over.

We told them that Brent had recently completed an evaluation to help determine if there was a neurological basis for his difficulties and that we had an appointment at the end of February to get another opinion and further evaluation, this time with a psychologist who was familiar with Asperger Syndrome and high-functioning autism. We agreed to share information if we found new ways to help Brent be more successful in the workplace following this evaluation. In the meantime, we explained that Brent had been diagnosed with ADHD, and that we found he had more success in a work environment with limited distractions and where instructions were clear and explicit. Moreover, we suggested that it would be helpful if the person giving the instructions would determine if Brent understood them before expecting him to start a task. Greg admitted that the company had been remiss in providing Brent with a clear job description and directions. Furthermore, since his previous boss, Sam, had left the company,

Brent had been working for several staff members who often gave conflicting directives, making it extremely difficult for him to prioritize the assignments. In addition, he shared an office with a vice president who continually interrupted him to ask basic computer questions. Greg apologized for the company's lack of organization and agreed that this had especially been a disservice to Brent.

Greg agreed to provide Brent with a quieter working space and with one boss, Clint, who would be responsible for supervising his work. He then invited Clint to join us and asked him if he would be willing to mentor Brent. Clint told us that he had five children of his own and enjoyed working with young adults. He agreed to be Brent's supervisor. We were pleased because he seemed to be a good personality match for Brent.

When Clint left the office, Greg and Max shared their concern over Brent's apparent interest in Internet sites displaying sex and pornography. Their latest company mission was to create a completely pornography-free Internet service to sell to their Christian clients. Brent had checked the web sites out several times at their request and had found that they were not yet pornography-free. However, they believed that he was also visiting the sites at other times, which troubled them. Greg was especially concerned because he had worked with individuals addicted to sex when he was a social worker, and had seen how this addiction often led to more serious behavior. Moreover, he emphasized that Ted Bundy, former convicted serial killer, reported that his criminal activity was a direct result of his exposure to pornography. The meeting ended on a more positive note with Greg and Max reiterating what a valued employee Brent was. Greg closed the meeting with a lengthy prayer.

I mulled the comment about Ted Bundy over in my mind and asked Dr. McCartney, Brent's psychologist, for his opinion of Greg's insinuation that Brent had a problem with pornography. Dr. McCartney replied that he did not believe Brent was addicted to pornography and felt that the Ted Bundy statement was an overreaction on Greg's part. Although he could not professionally divulge information about Brent, specifically not without his permission, he had a good rapport with Brent and felt he knew him well enough to say that he was not addicted to pornography. We agreed that pornography could be addicting and was not a healthy pastime, but we still wondered why Greg had made such an adamant statement relating Brent's curiosity about sex to heinous crimes.

Shortly after, an attractive woman Brent's age began talking with him at work and asked him if he would take her to a church event for young single adults. She did not want to go to the church social alone, but wanted him to accompany her so she could meet a young man she was interested in getting to know. After first telling her that he would take her, Brent changed his mind the next day. When he told her, she said that she would go alone. She continued to talk to Brent at work and later asked if he would go out with her. When he told her that he had a new girlfriend and already had a date, she asked him if they could double date. Brent declined, telling her that he wanted to spend time alone with his girlfriend.

The next week the same young woman passed Brent's work area while he was checking to see if all the pornography had been filtered from the web site, upon the request of one of the vice presidents. Brent said that she made a comment about the pictures on his computer screen to which he responded that she looked better than the woman on the monitor. He did not have any idea that this conversation was not appropriate in the workplace and was absolutely stunned when he was called into Max's office the next morning to find out that he was fired on the spot.

Brent came home at 9:30 that March morning crying – he had been fired and he did not understand what had happened. I was sick with the flu and was asleep when he rushed into my room sobbing and saying that he needed to talk. I felt terribly bad for him; he looked so hurt and was crying inconsolably. I am still not sure how he was able to drive home safely because he was very visibly upset. Greg had not been at the office that day. Further, when he ran into Clint in the parking lot as he was leaving, Clint asked him where he was going. Clint was shocked when Brent told him he had been fired and that Max had told him to never set foot on the premises again or he would call the police. Clint had not been informed of the situation and assured Brent that he would call him when he got further clarification.

In exploring the situation with us, Brent said that Max had yelled at him, saying that his behavior could be considered sexual harassment. Brent was so stunned at the accusations that he could not defend himself. He was not able to say that he was following directives from one of the vice presidents and was not acting inappropriately by looking at the site for his own pleasure, as Max had assumed. In fact, it had not occurred to Brent that Max did not realize that he had been asked to check the site by one of the vice presidents. I wonder if this was because of a "theory of mind" deficit that causes individuals with Asperger Syndrome to have difficulty understanding that other people have thoughts, intentions, and desires that are different from their own. When Max confronted Brent with the comment he had made about the young woman looking better than the model on the screen, Brent explained that the young woman "was egging him on," at which point Max lost control and ordered Brent never to return to the office again. He was told to leave immediately and was not even allowed to retrieve his belongings. As Brent relayed this story, he seemed completely bewildered as to the reason for Max's volatile reaction.

Press and I tried several times to contact Greg to find out what had happened. Greg had told us in front of Max at the meeting in January that Brent would never be fired. In fact, he had assured us that if there were ever any problems, we would be informed so we could work together to resolve them. Obviously, this was not the case! Brent's direct supervisor had not even been consulted regarding the decision to fire him. Instead, Max had taken it upon himself to unilaterally make this decision. Greg did eventually call us to say that he regretted that he had not been in the office to smooth out the situation. Moreover, he admitted that if he had been around, it probably would not have happened; however, he had to back the president's decision and could not reinstate Brent. Furthermore, he was unable to ask Brent to come back to work because this would upset Ned, who was giving them free rent. Ned also reportedly was responsible for the young woman he was sponsoring from overseas, the same woman who had complained about Brent to Max. Greg's responses did not seem as smooth as they had been in January. In fact, I was shocked that he told us that he did not want to upset Ned. Did he really think that his comments would cause us to sympathize with him?

Clint offered to meet Brent and me at the office early one evening after everyone else had gone home so Brent could pick up his belongings. Clint was apologetic about the ugly way in which the situation had been handled and agreed to write a letter of recommendation for Brent. He also told him that the staff prayed for him during the morning prayer meeting; in fact, someone had asked for prayer regarding his interest in pornography. Despite these seemingly kind gestures, Press and I thought the staff displayed a pious and "holier than thou" attitude by assuming that Brent had a problem with pornography.

I was soon to find out that the company had officially been declared bankrupt. Eight months later, Brent and I were contacted by a local TV investigative reporter who requested an interview with us about our experience with Greg's company. The FBI was investigating Greg and his company because it appeared as though he had swindled thousands of people out of millions of dollars. Press and I were angered and felt duped by Greg's earlier commitment to be Brent's mentor.

In the meantime, Brent continued to look in the newspaper and on the Internet for another job. While searching for a job, he applied for unemployment payments only to find out that there was no record of him having worked for Greg's company. That's when we learned that Greg had never paid Brent's unemployment insurance, state and federal taxes, or Social Security. In addition to fraudulently cashing Brent's checks for medical insurance, Greg had evaded paying the mandated taxes on his employees!

Brent finally found a clerical government job through a newspaper advertisement, and began working in June of 1998. The first few weeks, he seemed to have a difficult time getting to work. Several times I found him in bed in a fetal position with the blankets over his head at the time when he was supposed to be leaving for work in the afternoon. I coaxed him to go to work and even offered to drive him. During one of these episodes, Brent was able to tell me that he was feeling scared as he lay in bed. I asked him if talking to Dr. Rubin or Dr. McCartney would help. I also suggested that medicine designed specifically for anxiety might help. In the past, his response to suggestions such as these would have been to say no and continue to sleep with the blankets over his head. However, this time he said he would like to see Dr. Rubin. Fortunately, Dr. Rubin was able to meet with us that very afternoon. He prescribed an anti-anxiety medication that Brent could take whenever he felt anxious. Brent was even able to go into work later that evening. He took the medicine several times over the next six to eight weeks, but then insisted that he did not need it. He has not taken it since.

It was becoming more and more apparent that change and transitions were increasingly difficult for Brent. Brent thought he was having problems because of his work hours, which were 4:30 p.m. to 1 a.m. On the other hand, Press and I had thought he would do well working these hours because they were the hours when he was most alert and productive at home. While he often had difficulty getting up in the morning, he loved to stay up late and watch television and play on the computer. Therefore, we thought it would be more difficult for him to work the day shift. But Brent insisted that he missed his favorite television shows by working the evening shift, and claimed that he would be able to get to work much easier if he worked the day shift. Despite our suggestion that he try to work the evening shift a few weeks longer and then videotape the television programs that he missed, Brent asked his supervisor if he could be transferred to the day shift. This request was granted almost immediately.

Brent had gone out socially with a group of young single adults from work several times while he was on the evening shift. However, when he switched to the day shift, this was no longer possible because they were working when Brent was free. Brent had some difficulty working the long hours, and used up most of his accrued vacation hours when he was too tired to work a full shift. After a couple of months, he was moved to another position because there was not enough work for him at the previous one. His supervisor reportedly told him that the work had dropped off and that he would need to work in other areas. It seemed as though they were inventing things for him to do in an attempt to keep him busy. Brent became increasingly bored. Besides, he was uncomfortable working in the other areas because the environment was extremely chaotic and noisy and he missed an older gentleman who had befriended him at his previous workstation.

When he told his supervisors that he would rather have the time off than work where he was uncomfortable, his supervisor would not allow him to take time off even though the work tasks had dropped off. Instead, he was placed in data entry. He was soon reprimanded for talking too much, because it supposedly slowed his work rate. When he informed his supervisor that the other data entry workers also were talking, the response was that their talking did not slow down their work. Brent told us that he experienced difficulty focusing on the data entry work because he found it to be terribly boring.

At this time we asked Brent if the psychologist from the Regional Center who had diagnosed him with Asperger Syndrome could talk to his supervisor and the people at work to explain what Asperger Syndrome was so they could understand Brent better and make appropriate accommodations for him. When Brent was first hired, he wrote on his employment application that he had Asperger Syndrome, but he would not allow us to invite Jason, the psychologist who diagnosed him, to come to the workplace to talk about his condition. Brent also had a job coach through VR funding, but he did not want him to come to the workplace because he did not want to appear different. Besides, he thought he could handle the job on his own. He did allow the job coach to regularly call his supervisor to check on his performance and provide suggestions. During one of these conversations, the job coach had explained that Asperger Syndrome caused Brent to have difficulty maintaining attention to tasks. However, that was the extent of the supervisor's knowledge concerning Brent's difficulties.

After the latest episode, Brent agreed to allow Jason to come and discuss his condition. Jason was planning on calling Brent's supervisor during the second week of October to set an appointment. However, on October 8 Brent was assigned to use a computer to obtain a census tract number for employment applications. He acted impulsively that day and made a poor choice that cost him his job. He sent a network broadcast message to the users in the local area network saying that the computer network server would shut down in five minutes. Several minutes later, he was confronted by the supervisors and asked if he had sent the message. He admitted that he had but said that he did not mean any harm. He was reprimanded because he had caused several of the workers to shut down their computers, which led to lost work time. The administrator reported that he was wasting time and demonstrating untrustworthiness and unreliability at the workplace. Furthermore, he would probably be fired. Brent began crying as he tried to explain that he was bored and that he had acted impulsively, not maliciously. When he asked them not to fire him, he was told that the director would make that decision, and that he would be notified of the decision when it was made.

Brent went to work the next day, again apologized for his behavior, and asked if it would be possible to keep his job. His supervisor told him that the decision was out of his hands because the director, who had never personally met Brent, needed to make a ruling. Brent completed a full workday and went home for the weekend without knowing his fate. Since Monday was a state holiday, the office was closed. Brent reported for work on Tuesday as usual, and still no decision had been made. Ten minutes before the end of the workday, Brent was notified that he was fired.

As a consequence of his impulsive behavior at work, the State Department of Unemployment Insurance denied him unemployment benefits. We tried to explain that impulsivity was part of Brent's disability and was not reflective of maliciousness. Moreover, appropriate accommodations had not been made to address his disability – he had been put into work situations where he was uncomfortable and was not able to perform at his optimum level. We decided to make a formal complaint about the manner in which Brent had been fired. It was during this complaint process that we found out more specifics about Brent's work behavior.

Documentation from Brent's employment file revealed that he had broken the five-minute phone rule several times and had been confronted about this infraction. His supervisor explained that when he timed Brent, he found that he was on the phone for personal reasons one time for 12 minutes and another time for 23 minutes when he was supposed to be working. An attractive young woman from the evening shift was calling him. Brent responded to the supervisor by saying that he did not break the rule and that he hung the phone up after five minutes and then called her back. The supervisor documented that he thought Brent was playing a game with him. However, this type of behavior is characteristic of individuals with Asperger Syndrome. When they interpret rules literally, it often appears as though they are trying to manipulate the situation when, in fact, they believe that they are just following the rules.

It was also documented that Brent reported that three other employees told him to obey the rules because they were planning to file a complaint against the supervisor. They had explained to Brent that the supervisor had to document everything that happened and if Brent did not obey, the records could be used against him after they officially filed their complaint. Apparently, Brent did not realize that the three employees told him this information in confidence and that their intention to file a complaint was not to be shared with the supervisor. In hindsight this appears to be another example of how individuals with Asperger Syndrome miss social cues and the more subtle nuances of conversation and relationships. In addition, Brent had also told his supervisor that he thought some of the rules at work were stupid, that he thought he was being singled out and treated unfairly, that he did not like being told what he needed to do at work, that he sometimes purposely chose not to work in response to their reprimands, and that he liked to be rebellious.

This rebellious behavior was in direct contrast to the compliant and cooperative behavior Brent had demonstrated toward his teachers throughout his high school years. At 22 years of age Brent acted more like an adolescent than when he actually was an adolescent. However, his behavior is understandable when one considers that Asperger Syndrome is a developmental disability. That is, Brent was acting in a manner that was more characteristic of an individual two-thirds his chronological age – precisely the behavior characteristic of an adolescent! It must have been extremely difficult for Brent to be physically 22 years old, and yet have the social and emotional maturity equivalent to a person many years younger. Most people he came in contact with, including us, expected him to act similarly to his chronological-age peers, but he was not able to. In addition, he did not understand his own behavior and was unable to tell us how he felt.

It appears that what determines whether or not people keep their positions in today's job market depends more on their social skills and their ability to get along with co-workers than on their technical job-related skills. Given that Asperger Syndrome adversely affects social and communication skills, individuals with this condition are at an extreme disadvantage. Brent was unable to maintain employment basically because of his difficulty with social skills. He did not understand the unwritten rules and did not have the social savvy to be successful. Brent's last supervisor wrote in his work file that he believed Brent demonstrated difficulties with attention because he did not want to work. It is so incredibly difficult to convince people who are not familiar with this disability that individuals with Asperger Syndrome truly have difficulty focusing on what is relevant, often experience anxiety, and frequently do not know how to express their feelings. They are not purposely trying to be belligerent or lazy, although their behavior may look as though that is the case. I truly believe that the pain they cause others is never greater than the pain they themselves experience.

After going through this discouraging episode, Press thought that Brent's self-esteem might improve if he could work at a job that was not stressful and where he felt valued and accepted. When Press was shopping at our local supermarket one day, he asked Brent's former manager if he needed any help, especially during the holiday season. He went on to say that Brent was currently between jobs. Lon encouraged Press to ask Brent to apply to work at the supermarket. I was concerned that working with the public might be too challenging for Brent; however, Press thought that Brent would feel comfortable at the supermarket because Lon had always been very kind to him and the place was familiar to him. As a result, by the end of November, Brent started working part-time at the supermarket near our home.

Several days after he started working, Brent was told that they needed cashiers, and that they wanted to train him for that position. Even though he occasionally had to work with a difficult customer as a cashier, Brent, at first, did not think it was too difficult, because when those situations arose he just called for the manager to talk with the customer. I thought this was a successful strategy that he figured out on his own. However, he did say that being responsible for the cash register was very stressful. In fact, he would rather have worked as a sacker than as a cashier. But the managers insisted that they needed him to work as a cashier because they had enough sackers. The other sackers were typically too young to be hired as cashiers.

Soon, Brent began staying in bed and telling us that he did not feel well enough to go to work. We were not sure if he was truly physically sick or if he was so anxious that it caused him to feel ill. One time when he called the supermarket office, one of the older women asked him in a sarcastic manner if he was calling in sick again. Brent realized that she was making fun of him, and he felt bad. He resigned from his position as cashier in March of 1999 and did not work again for two years. In the meantime, he did some volunteer computer work at the Regional Center, which was later created into an unpaid internship. It was our hope, and the social service case manager's hope, that Brent would learn some of the necessary employment social skills in an environment that was accepting of his condition. After all, he was a client of the Regional Center. If any facility was familiar with his disability, they sure were. Brent volunteered at the Regional Center until he started school full-time in November of 1999.

Brent graduated as a computer technician in January of 2001 and worked with a vocational counselor for eight months trying to secure employment. After a six-month search in the computer field, he still had not been able to secure a job. His advisor at the computer training program comforted him by saying that they had not placed any graduates in new jobs during the first five months of the year because numerous companies had gone out of business.

Brent decided to expand his search and look for alternative part-time employment. He tried to work as a security guard, but only completed two days of training. Both his vocational counselor and I spoke to his supervisor, who noted that Brent was doing well during the training. However, Brent could not tolerate the work. The required contact with people in sometimes confrontational situations was not a good fit.

As of this writing, Brent has just started working as an administrative clerk for a non-profit organization that provides housing for individuals with developmental disabilities. I found out about the position through one of the professionals who worked with Brent in the past. Since his employment is funded through limited grant money, the organization could only offer him five hours of work per week. He has successfully completed his first six weeks of employment under the supervision of his vocational job coach. This organization was willing to hear about Brent's strengths and weaknesses before they interviewed him. Although his job coach's contract to help Brent find a job is technically over, she is committed to help him until he is successfully acclimated in his new job. She has been an answer to our prayers.

We had hoped that by this time Brent would be working 20 to 25 hours a week using his computer skills. However, we can only take one day at a time and handle each new challenge as it comes. We are grateful that he is employed through the help of VR with an organization that understands his disability and is willing to give him a chance. They also allow him flexibility in scheduling his hours because of his continued difficulty waking up early in the morning if he has not been able to sleep well the previous night. Who knows where this will lead? We continue to pray that Brent will feel valued, supported, and understood at his job.

Lessons Learned

It appears that Temple Grandin's advice regarding employment for individuals with Asperger Syndrome could not be more accurate. Jobs involving significant interaction with other people can be very anxiety-provoking and stressful because of all the subtle social nuances and unspoken rules. Instead, Temple recommends a position where the individual works independently on assigned projects most of the time with limited interaction with others. When I heard her speak at the annual Autism Society of America Conference in July of 1999, she stated that being a cashier was one of the worst occupations for individuals with Asperger Syndrome. From experience, I agree, and so does Brent!

Also, I now see that although Brent could not always express his anxiety in words, he was continuously giving us clues through nonverbal behavior that we either dismissed or thought we could help him overcome. Brent's behavior and his words were conveying that he needed more structure, modeling of a work task, and a chance to show whether or not he understood the directions before he began working on the assigned task independently. Furthermore, he needed a less distracting environment, shorter workdays, and fewer face-to-face interactions with others. He was unable to read office politics and interpret others' intentions. A work environment in which the employer and employees are educated about Asperger Syndrome and how it affects Brent before he begins working and making social blunders is probably the most beneficial support that can be provided.

References

Romoser, M. (2000). Malemployment in autism. *Focus on Autism and Other Developmental Disabilities, 15,* 246-247.

chapter eight

Perseverative and Obsessive Interests

B rent's interest in computers and the Internet reached perseverative and obsessive heights in college. He still avidly pursues this interest seven years later, making this the longest lasting obsession he has consistently followed. Several years ago Brent's extreme sense of curiosity led him to continually try new things on the computer. Sometimes he would become so involved in this process that his impulsivity and compulsivity caused him to compromise the integrity of the Microsoft Windows Operating System. When he reached that point, he needed to reformat the entire hard drive, which resulted in wiping out the entire system. At this juncture, he would begin rebuilding the operating system and all of the application software from scratch. On several occasions, he stayed up throughout the night to complete the process. It was essential to him to do so because he needed to regain Internet access and reinstall the games and music programs he had worked long and hard to set up!

Twice he unplugged his computer and deposited it in our family room with a note saying that he could not deal with computers, never wanted to work with them again, and wanted us to take his computer system out of the house. Computers were Brent's life, so these situations must have been very painful for him. We did not remove the computer from the house, but suggested that when he got frustrated while trying to fix it, he should stop and watch television or visit a friend and then start working on it again once he was no longer so agitated. He promised that he would not stay up again throughout the night to work on his computer, admitting that he probably made more mistakes when he was tired and frustrated. However, once Brent started fixing his computer, he found it very hard to walk away and let go of the situation. Perseverance to see a task through to its completion is a positive quality, but Brent seemed to go beyond that point to engage in destructive and self-defeating behaviors.

During that same year, Brent discovered that one of our neighbors, Rob, bought used computers and upgraded them. Soon Brent purchased a modem and more memory capability from Rob. Press and Brent also called Rob several times to fix the damage Brent had done while experimenting with his computer. These were very painful times for all of us. Press would become frustrated when he found out that Brent's computer was completely cleared of all of its programs, the programs Brent had spent weeks creating. He then felt bad and called Rob to ask if he could fix the computer again. Shortly after Rob decided to dissolve his business, Brent began taking his computer to a local store for upgrades and repairs. Fortunately, the frequency of these repairs has significantly decreased, and Brent now just periodically upgrades his computer.

When Brent was working for the government, he began purchasing software over uBid sites on the Internet. He found deals that were too good to pass up, even though he did not need the software, and in some cases already had a copy of it. His compulsiveness seemed to have reached new heights and he was unable to stop himself. He spent hours on the computer checking to see if his bid was accepted. The uBid sites made it easy for him to make purchases by just requiring his bank debit card number.

Press and I were torn about how much we should be involved in this buying frenzy. After all, most parents of 22-year-olds did not interfere with their adult child's finances. However, we also felt that this behavior was similar to an addiction and wanted Brent to learn to monitor his own behavior. As a compromise, we asked Brent to talk to us about any purchase he wanted to make on the Internet that was over $25 so we could make a joint decision. Brent agreed. However, he still seemed to be making many purchases, as evidenced by the frequency of the UPS truck stopping at our home. Brent defended his behavior by pointing out that even though the frequency of these purchases did not decrease, he was now buying most items for under $25.

During that summer, I had major surgery. Unfortunately, I developed complications and needed to stay in the hospital several days longer than expected. When I arrived home, I was still feeling miserable and spent a lot of time in my nightgown on the couch. My mother came up from Florida for about a week to help as I recovered. About 10 o'clock every weekday morning the doorbell would ring and the same gentleman from UPS would deliver several packages addressed to Brent. I had never met the man before because I was usually working when he made his deliveries. My mother observed that this 10 o'clock knock on the front door was becoming a ritual. As I started feeling better, I commented to the delivery person that I normally did not hang around the house in my nightgown all day, but I had surgery and was not feeling well. He just smiled and asked if Brent was starting his own business since he was delivering computer items to our home almost daily. The truth of the matter was that Brent was just purchasing items he could not resist because they were such a bargain!

One evening at about 10 o'clock, Brent came upstairs and asked me to help him with a problem. He spoke very softly because he did not want his dad to hear. Whenever he does not want Press to know about something, I immediately get suspicious. I imagine he thinks that I am more of a pushover than his dad; besides, he does not like to disappoint his dad. He had found VCRs advertised on the Internet at a phenomenal price and wanted to order two of them. They were about $35 each – with shipping and handling the total cost would be about $50 a piece. I could understand that

Brent wanted to replace the old VCR we had given him, because he had been complaining for some time that it was not working well. But I did not understand why he needed to buy two identical VCRs. To my horror, he added that he thought he pressed the "2" key on the computer when he ordered the VCRs, but he must have pressed it twice because the company was in the process of sending him 22 VCRs.

I suggested that Brent call the company first thing in the morning to explain the error. But it wasn't that simple. Brent had made the mistaken purchase at 6 o'clock that evening and had already called the company after receiving their confirmation of the purchase, which is when he realized the mistake. Supposedly, he was told that he could not change his mind and that the order was already being processed. Panicking because he did not want 22 VCRs coming to our house, Brent cleverly figured that if he gave a bogus address they would not be able to deliver them, and he would be off the hook. He showed me the confirmation that the VCRs were going to what Brent thought was a fictitious address in town. I had visions of someone actually living at this address and being surprised by this windfall of free merchandise paid for by Brent's debit card!

I told Brent that I thought there was a law to protect consumers that allowed them up to 72 hours after making a purchase to back out of the deal without a penalty. Brent insisted that the person he had talked with over the phone was very forceful and had firmly declared that the order could not be changed and that he needed to accept all 22 VCRs. I then reminded Brent that he would still be paying for the computers even if they went to a bogus address because the company had his debit card number and would probably be withdrawing the money from his checking account the next morning. We checked to see if he had enough money in his account to cover the 22 VCRs. He had $773, just enough to cover the VCRs without the shipping and handling charges.

At this point, I suggested that he withdraw as much money that evening as the 24-hour ATM machine would allow. I thought they only allowed a maximum of $300 each withdrawal. Then I said that we needed to go to the bank when they opened the next morning, explain the situation and ask them to put a stop payment on the company trying to collect for the VCRs and possibly close the account.

Finally, I told Brent that his dad needed to know about this and that he might have a better solution. I was not sure what should be done. I was pretty sure that the company had given Brent misinformation in an attempt to coerce him to buy the VCRs. Press did not have any other suggestions, so Brent left by himself to withdraw his money from the ATM machine at 10:30 that evening. Surprisingly, he came home with $770.

The next morning Brent and I went to the bank to explain the situation. We were told that he could not be forced to accept the 22 VCRs and that the bank would watch for the withdrawal request and not allow it. In addition, they suggested that Brent close his account and open up a new one with the $770 cash. Since we told Brent the night before that having a debit card was probably not a wise idea for him at this time, he informed the bank administrator that he no longer wanted a debit card because it made it too easy for him to order items over the Internet. As a further precaution, she suggested that in addition to not having a debit card, he not order an ATM card with his new checking account. I was not sure that we wanted him to be that restricted, since having that card would allow him to withdraw and deposit money at times when the bank was not open. I did not want to give him money when he needed it by lending it to him or asking him to write me a check. Of course, I would do that for him in a pinch, but I did not want him to feel as though he were back in junior high school when he received allowances from us. Brent decided to request an ATM card with his new checking account and to decline the debit card.

As we left the bank, Brent said, "Mom, couldn't you tell something was wrong when the UPS man kept coming to our house? Why didn't you stop me?" I reminded him that I was sick at the time and was barely able to care for myself. Furthermore, I told him that it sounded as if he wanted me to put brakes on his behavior, and yet he frequently got upset when we tried to do just that. Battling between wanting to break away from parents and wanting their support is the struggle of adolescence. Press and I were constantly struggling to find the best way to parent Brent. We wanted him to be independent, and part of that meant we needed to step back and allow him to make mistakes. We did not, and still do not, want to run his life. On the other hand, parents can easily fall into the role of being more protective and somewhat enabling when they have a child with a disability who requires more structure and assistance. I shared with Brent that we continually try to determine where the boundary lines are in our relationship with him.

Although we had agreed that Brent should keep his ATM card, we were mildly concerned that he withdrew money on a frequent basis when he became fixated on buying something. A short-lived interest in baseball cards reemerged, and over a period of 10 days he spent $350 on baseball cards, stopping at the bank to withdraw $50 each time. He had no idea that he had spent that much in such a short period of time. We only realized it when we asked him to balance his checkbook. He had not recorded any of these withdrawals, and as a result did not realize how much money he had spent. I think he was also shocked because the cost of baseball cards had increased significantly since his teenage years when he was an avid collector, and the small stack of new cards he had accumulated did not seem to be worth $350.

In the same vein, Brent later admitted that he had been stopping at the gambling boat on the way home from his evening computer classes to play video poker. Apparently, these quarter poker games had added up quickly, too. We discussed how this behavior could be addicting and suggested that Brent make a decision not to go to the boats at all since it was so difficult for him to stop himself from putting money in the machines. If this choice was not realistic for him, then he needed to consider only going occasionally with no more than $10 or $20 in his pocket to limit his spending. We also explained that the gambling machines were designed for the establishment to make money, not the patrons, and that the machines were programmed to allow occasional wins to keep people interested in playing. Furthermore, this can be especially dangerous for the addictive personality. Brent did change his behavior. As a result, he met a friend for dinner and went to the casino with a $10 limit. However, when the friend confessed to a similar problem, they decided not to go to the boats for entertainment anymore.

Apparently, this resolve lasted for a considerable length of time. This was quite an accomplishment, considering that the casino was conveniently located on the road he traveled to get to and from school four times a week. However, one Saturday night his friend called to meet him for dinner at the casino, and they decided to play on the poker and slot machines. The friend went home by 11, but Brent stayed on to play for a few more minutes. These few minutes soon turned into two hours, which included several trips to the ATM machine located inside the casino. This machine charged extra fees, which Brent did not realize until he received his monthly checking account statement. Evidently, Brent lost $90, plus extra ATM charges, that evening. He told us the next day that he was so disgusted with himself that he cut the ATM card into little pieces and threw it out the car window as he drove home from the casino.

I thought that he had figured out a clever way to put external limits on himself, given his extreme difficulty in setting internal limits. Press was not as pleased with his behavior, emphasizing to Brent the dangers of gambling and how it can become addictive and destroy individuals and their families. Both of us had expressed concern numerous times over Brent's proclivity toward addictive behavior. However, his interest in gambling was certainly looking like an addiction. Brent describes this behavior as impulsive and has told both us and his psychiatrist that for him this is the most bothersome problem associated with Asperger Syndrome to cope with.

In the meantime, Brent avidly pursued opportunities on the Internet to win money and prizes that did not involve the expenditure of money. For instance, he played Instant Win games that included scratch-off cards, slot machines, and occasionally poker. He believed that this pastime was acceptable because he was not actually gambling with money. Press and I still thought it was an addiction and that Brent spent too much of his free time immersed in this pursuit. Our hope was that he would soon realize that this was not a good use of his time after he did not win anything. However, this turned out to be much more profitable than the gambling boat! Unfortunately, the winnings Brent began collecting further reinforced this habit, so he continued to put more and more of his time into this activity. Despite hearing from us and his psychiatrist that although he was making money, he could not live independently just on his earnings from Instant Win games and entering contests on the computer, he continued to devote excessive hours to this interest. Brent assured us that he understood and that when he obtained a job after completing his Vatterott College training, he would have to cut back significantly on his computer time and start considering it as a hobby. However, he is currently not engaged in full-time employment and still spends a considerable amount of his free time on the Internet.

Brent began receiving checks valued from $1 to $5 in the mail as a result of winning an Instant Win game or as compensation for completing a survey over the Internet. Then the free products began arriving on an almost daily basis. In fact, they are still arriving! It has been amazing to see how much money companies spend on postage and delivery for the small items they send as free promotions. For example, Brent received a small bottle of maple syrup about 3 inches in height that cost the company $3.20 to send him Priority Mail! For several weeks we received boxes containing small snacks, such as a tiny bag of potato chips and one individually wrapped Lifesaver™ in each box. Over several months' time, Brent received more than 20 white T-shirts with the logo of the company that sent it imprinted on the front. Brent still proudly wears these shirts. When Brent found a site that offered free running shoes, he promptly ordered a pair, which soon arrived at our home. He proceeded to tell his brother-in-law about the site so he could order a pair, too. When I saw their new running shoes at Christmas, I jokingly asked Brent if he could order a pair for me. Unfortunately, the promotion was over.

This obsession reached new heights when Brent was awarded $500 from Publisher's Clearinghouse. No, Ed McMahon did not come to our door with his camera crew to award Brent the money. Press and I were initially very skeptical about this windfall, thinking that Brent might have misunderstood the situation. However, Brent did receive a letter in the mail congratulating him, along with a check for $500. The check was real, and he was able to cash it. Around the same time, Brent also received notification that he had won a GPS III Palm pilot specifically for aircraft from an Internet site. None of our family members or friends owns a plane or has a pilot's license, so the item was of no use to Brent or us. Brent resourcefully advertised this brand-new prize over the Internet and received over $300 for it. Reportedly, the item was worth over $500. His other big windfall came from playing a lotto game on-line for which he received a $300 check.

Although Brent stopped going to the casinos to gamble, he substituted this activity by playing arcade games whenever possible. The five months that he dated Melinda, his last serious girlfriend, they frequently went to a Family Fun Center that had miniature golf and arcades. Here he won many inexpensive stuffed toys for Melinda. But since he was not keeping track of how much money he was withdrawing from the ATM machine, he had no idea that they spent almost $100 during one weekend just at the arcades. They certainly had not accumulated $100 worth of stuffed toys! Brent realized that he could have purchased Melinda several nice stuffed animals for far less than $100; however, then he would not have had the "fun" of trying to win them.

As of this writing Brent has not been to the arcades or gambling boats for entertainment for probably a year. However, he still avidly plays Instant Win games, enters contests, completes surveys for compensation, uses chat lines to talk to and meet women, and looks for free merchandise on the Internet. He recently won $50 and a Sony Walkman TV Tuner AM/FM Stereo Cassette Player from two different Internet sites. He has his daily search routine for free items down to a science so that if he is limited in time, he can complete these numerous searches in 30 minutes. This search ritual is important to Brent because the highlight of his day is waiting for the mail to be delivered so he can see what free merchandise he has won. When he is home, he watches for our mail carrier and actually starts to pace in front of the window when she is running late because he is anxious to see what will be delivered.

Lessons Learned

The perseverative and compulsive tendencies characteristic of individuals with Asperger Syndrome may lead to addictive behaviors. These characteristics, combined with Brent's impulsive nature, have made it difficult for him to control some of his behavior. Discussing these situations with Brent before they get out of control has not always been helpful. He has still needed to learn from his own mistakes, sometimes making the same mistake over and over. As a parent, it is difficult to watch this from the sidelines and not intervene to head off disaster. Several times Brent has become defiant, demanding that we give him space to lead his own life; at other times he has asked us why we did not stop him when we saw he was getting out of control. Discussing this dilemma of knowing when to intervene and when not to with Brent's therapist has helped resolve some of the issues. Setting up the ground rules together as a family has made it easier to implement them without emotional involvement.

But this situation is still not resolved. Impulsive activities can occur at any time and regression to previous activities can also happen. Currently, we are wondering whether bipolar disorder is possibly a comorbid condition that may be impacting Brent's moods and desire to engage in risk-taking behaviors without regard for the possible consequences.

chapter nine

Depression
and Anxiety

We first became keenly aware that Brent was struggling emotionally, but was unable to tell us, in February of 1997, when he was commuting to DeVry and working part-time. Press and I were attending different conferences over the weekend, leaving Brent home alone for about 30 hours. I had been invited to stay longer in St. Louis with a friend after the conference was over on Saturday, but I had a gnawing feeling that I had better get back home. I was not exactly sure why I felt the need to get back home, but I was soon to find out.

While at the conference, I tried to call Brent several times before he was supposed to go to work at McDonald's early Friday evening. There was no answer. This was not unusual. Brent frequently did not answer the phone when he was sound asleep, so I didn't worry. Press and I had left telephone numbers where we could be reached if Brent needed to contact us. Neither of us heard from him.

When I got home late Saturday evening, I found Brent in bed. When I asked him how the last two days had been, he told me that he had taken some Tylenol the day before, but could not remember how many. He was unable to describe how he felt then or how he was feeling as we spoke. He looked alert, but indicated that he had spent almost the entire time I had been away in bed. He had not gone to work, nor had he called work to tell them that he would not be in. Brent had never made a suicide attempt before, nor had he ever communicated a wish to die. He told me that he did not know why he took the Tylenol; he just wanted to see what would happen. He denied feelings of sadness and was unable to provide any information that would explain why he took the Tylenol. Even though he appeared alert and coherent, I called Poison Control. Following their recommendation, I immediately took him to the hospital emergency room because they said Tylenol could cause irreversible liver damage if it was not treated within 24 hours. Brent's story suggested that 24 hours had probably already elapsed, but he did not know for sure how many pills he had ingested. Fortunately, blood tests revealed that he did not have any liver damage, so we were able to return home about 3 o'clock the next morning.

That whole evening seemed incredibly surreal. I kept wishing that Press were home to share this scary and confusing time with us and to help process all that had transpired. I was exhausted mentally and physically after sitting in conferences for the previous two days and then driving for over four hours to get home. On the drive back, all I could think of was climbing into bed and sleeping until late the next morning. It is amazing how one's body can change from a state of utter exhaustion to an adrenaline-pumped machine when needed. However, the exhaustion did catch up with me, and I was able to finally get to sleep around 4:30 a.m. Sunday. What also seemed surreal to me was Brent's amazing calmness through the entire emergency room experience. He seemed very quiet and calm, and his affect was rather flat. His almost complete lack of emotion throughout this whole ordeal was very bewildering to me.

The doctor on call for Dr. Rubin, Brent's psychiatrist, had reportedly been called by the hospital emergency room while we were there; however, he did not call to follow up with Brent on Sunday. Once the crisis was over, Brent seemed to be back to his usual self, so I did not call the psychiatrist on call but decided instead to call Dr. Rubin Monday morning to tell him about Brent's weekend and share my concerns about his recent behavior. I was immediately allowed to speak to Dr. Rubin and we set up an appointment to see him that afternoon. I was anxious to talk to him because, except for sleeping a lot, which Brent had always been good at, he did not indicate that he was depressed. I assumed he had to be depressed to take an overdose of Tylenol. Dr. Rubin asked Brent to describe what had led to his decision to take Tylenol, but Brent could only respond that he did not know and that he just wanted to see what it felt like. Dr. Rubin questioned him further to assess if he had a suicide plan. Brent denied having a plan and promised to continue taking his medication.

Professionally, I had worked with high school students who had contemplated and even attempted suicide while working as a school counselor and as a school psychologist. Press and I had not observed any of those classic suicidal behaviors in Brent. He never tried to give away valued possessions, engage in high-risk behavior, or talk about death or suicide. Again, we were baffled and wondered if there was any way that this could have been prevented. While talking to Dr. Rubin, I casually mentioned that I had been to a conference on autism while Brent was home and had noted that Brent demonstrated so many of the characteristics of this disorder. Nevertheless, we both agreed that Brent did not have classic autism, and the subject was dismissed. Dr. Rubin did indicate that he believed Brent's learning difficulties and problems in communicating his feelings were significantly impacting him. However, the possibility of an autism spectrum disorder (ASD), such as Asperger Syndrome, was not suggested at that time.

As mentioned in Chapter Six, Brent began skipping classes, lying to us about it, and sleeping frequently during the afternoons shortly after the Tylenol incident when he was in his third semester at DeVry. He denied feelings of depression and continued to take the antidepressant medication prescribed. However, he often needed to be reminded to take his medicine. Around this time, I found a psychologist, Dr. McCartney, who was highly recommended by Dr. Rubin because of his work with college students. We were very concerned about Brent and hoped that maybe someone else could help him communicate what was troubling him since he was not able to tell us. Again, I assumed something was bothering him given the incident with Tylenol, but he did not verbalize that anything was disturbing him. Moreover, his appetite appeared to be good most of the time, although he tended to eat a lot of foods high in fat content. Brent agreed to try counseling again, and began seeing Dr. McCartney in early May of 1997. This counseling relationship continued for several years.

Before Brent began to develop the great rapport he later came to share with Dr. McCartney, he experienced another crisis. When I came home from work on Friday, May 17, 1997 – approximately three months after the Tylenol incident – I found that Brent had not gone to school. He said that he had spent most of the day in bed. A couple of hours later Brent came downstairs to show me what he had been doing in his room. What I saw as Brent approached me was an extremely bloody arm. In a somewhat blasé and flippant manner, Brent said that he had wanted to see what it felt like to cut his arm with a pocketknife. He held his head high, walked with his shoulders back, and strutted past me toward the kitchen. This behavior was very uncharacteristic of Brent. The flippant attitude still occasionally arises, but not the self-injurious behavior. I was not sure how deep the cuts were by looking at his blood-soaked arm. I calmly asked him to come over to the sink so I could clean his arm.

I remember telling myself to be calm and pretend that Brent was a patient and not my son so I could cope better with the situation. I had taken care of many accident victims while working as a nurse in a hospital emergency room before Brent was born and knew that I could clean and bandage his arm if I did not think about it too much. Again, I felt as if the whole experience was surreal. I did what I needed to do to help Brent while acting like a robot. If I had let my emotions take over, I would probably not have been able to handle the immediate crisis. I cleaned his arm and told him we needed to call his psychiatrist to get him help. Brent just nodded. I was relieved that the numerous cuts were only superficial and were mostly on his forearm, not on his wrist.

Press came home from playing golf shortly after I had cleaned Brent's arm and was just as horrified as I to learn what Brent had done. Neither of us had any idea what had led Brent to react in this manner. In fact, we still do not know for sure. While waiting for Dr. Rubin to return my call, we searched for the specifics about our medical insurance coverage so we could share it with him. Brent was quiet and docile and asked if he could rest for a while. Dr. Rubin phoned us immediately after being notified by his answering service of our call. He recommended we admit Brent to the hospital for observation. About 45 minutes later, after speaking to the hospital admitting office and a social worker, we woke Brent up to tell him that we needed to take him to the hospital for his safety and to get him help. He let us pack some clothing and toiletries for him and voluntarily got into the car to go with us. In the meantime, as we drove to the hospital, Dr. Rubin phoned a colleague who agreed to be Brent's admitting psychiatrist and to provide him with background information on Brent. Dr. Rubin told him that Brent had been his patient for three years and that he believed he experienced problems communicating that might stem from his learning disability in addition to his inattentiveness, which he had been treating pharmacologically for the past three years.

Curt, a social worker from the adult psychiatric unit, greeted us when we arrived at the hospital. Curt was reassuring and asked numerous questions to assess Brent's mental status as well as to determine what had led to the current crisis. Brent continually looked toward us for answers. He appeared confused and dull, and seemed to display a rather flat affect. However, this type of response was not totally unusual for Brent. Whenever we had been to doctors in the past, he frequently looked to me or Press to supply the answers to their questions. He denied any auditory or visual hallucinations and paranoia; however, he could not identify a precipitating factor for his self-injurious behavior and would not state that he would not harm himself. We were not sure that he understood the gravity of what he had just done and why the hospital staff needed to exercise extreme caution due to his inability to say that he would not try to harm himself again. He was checked every 15 minutes by the hospital staff as a precaution until the admitting doctor arrived the next day.

Curt informed us that most of Brent's ratings on the mental status checklist fell within the mild range; however, he rated Brent as moderately guarded, sad, depressed, and having poor judgment. His also rated Brent's mood and affect as severely bewildered. As Brent was being interviewed by the nurse, Curt candidly told us that the admitting physician wanted to rule out possible psychosis, given Brent's staring into space, sudden change of behavior, and inability to provide much information regarding his mood and feelings.

I remember commenting to Curt and Press prior to leaving the hospital that night how this hospital was so much more pleasant and not as intimidating as the psychiatric ward where I trained as a registered nurse over 20 years earlier. The psychiatric ward where I worked was very old, had bright-yellow enameled walls, and was a locked unit. It looked just like the hospital in the movie "One Flew Over the Cuckoo's Nest." It was not a place where you wanted to leave a family member! Before we left, we told Brent that we would see him the next day and wished him a restful night's sleep.

When Press and I left the hospital close to midnight, we drove home quietly, each silent in our own thoughts. The only recollection I have of the later part of that evening is a feeling of numbness. Brent was compliant and docile. He did not appear scared to be left at the hospital, although he had never been a hospital patient before, except at birth. But it was such an unnerving feeling to leave our son at a psychiatric unit. Press and I had never imagined that we would need to hospitalize Brent in order to protect him. Although Brent voluntarily signed the hospital admittance papers, he merely seemed to be following directions without much understanding of what was happening.

When we arrived the next day during visiting hours, we were told that we could accompany Brent to the dining room for dinner. He was now in a regular room because he had stated that he would not harm himself. He reportedly told his nurse that he had not planned to cut his arm the previous evening and that he just did it impulsively. He still could not identify any precipitating factors, however.

The staff members were friendly and the hospital unit appeared to be cheerful, safe, and nonthreatening. Nevertheless, I still remember feeling rather numb and wondering how Brent was interpreting this whole sequence of events. During our visit we played cards and talked to Brent about what he had done during the day. He had spent most of the time in his room reading and studying his computer books. We promised that we would call the owner of the company that Brent worked for part-time as a computer programmer, as he requested, to ask for some leave time until he felt ready to return. We also discussed his school situation and decided to ask for a medical withdrawal until Brent could better determine what he wanted to do.

Several days after Brent's admission, Press and I asked if we could meet with the admitting psychiatrist because we wanted to share our concerns and find out what the professionals believed was at the root of Brent's difficulties. Brent was compliant at the hospital, but he did not speak much and was described as isolative during the first days of his six-day hospitalization. Press and I provided the psychiatrist with a detailed developmental history of Brent, including his social and communication difficulties and his special education history. Press also shared his concerns about

Brent's perseverative interests, particularly the intensity of these interests and the abrupt abandoning of the baseball card interest. The psychiatrist replied that maybe Brent would become another Bill Gates given his current computer interest. This comment was not comforting or helpful to us, although perhaps intended to be so. He also indicated that I appeared to be an overcompensating mother. Furthermore, he expressed frustration because Brent barely spoke to him. He indicated that Dr. Rubin believed this might be because Brent had communication difficulties related to his learning disability. The diagnosis of Asperger Syndrome was not suggested.

The prescribed treatment for Brent at the hospital was a trial dose of a new medication to treat depression and help stabilize his mood along with group therapy. Brent did not attend one of the earlier therapy sessions and, by his own and staff reports, when he did attend he hardly spoke and needed much coaxing to share his thoughts. Brent was the youngest adult on the unit. He told us that most other patients shared their feelings freely. Most of them were dealing with issues much different from his, although one other young adult was also dealing with depression.

By the fifth day, Brent was repeatedly asking when he could go home, so we tried to find out what the treatment plan was and how much longer he would need to stay at the hospital. Curt, the social worker, informed us that he would probably need to stay through the weekend. We were disappointed, because not much in the way of treatment or diagnostic procedures happen over the weekend. Moreover, except for a physical examination and some blood work, no other diagnostic tests were done or were even being planned. Furthermore, Brent was no longer suicidal, so what was the purpose of extending his stay? We had hoped that they would have conducted some neurological testing to shed light on what was happening with Brent.

Press contacted the admitting psychiatrist again to find out what the treatment plan was and how long Brent would need to be an inpatient. The psychiatrist again expressed frustration that Brent was not talking much in the group counseling, stating that he probably would not be able to go home until he talked more about his thoughts and feelings. After Curt shared this with Brent, he began to talk more during the group session later that day. Press also shared with the admitting psychiatrist that the $10,000 mental health coverage our medical insurance allowed for the year was almost exhausted after five days. Interestingly, after Press shared this information, the admitting psychiatrist decided that Brent was well enough to go home that evening. It is amazing and rather sad how influential our medical insurance can be in determining treatment.

Brent was scheduled to attend a partial hospital day program for the next two weeks and to continue therapy with his new therapist, Dr. McCartney. The partial hospital program involved group counseling sessions for approximately six hours per day, several times a week. Brent attended the program, although rather reluctantly at times. During this two-week program, he received an emergency card with a number to call if he ever felt as though he wanted to harm himself in the future. He continued to deny any further thoughts of suicide. But after being prompted, he did articulate that when he felt like isolating himself, this might be a warning that he was headed for a crisis. He also indicated that possible signs of relapse for him included anxiety, unexpressed feelings, and frustration with his progress. This information was reportedly reviewed with him during the partial hospital program. Again, Brent would not share much about his thoughts and feelings with us when he got home from these outpatient group therapy sessions.

Following his hospitalization we requested Brent's hospital records, with his permission. Since he was over 18, he needed to sign the record release. When the records arrived, Brent had no interest in seeing them, and told us that we could have them. Although the records contained some inaccuracies, most of what we had reported to Curt and the psychiatrist was included. Among other things, it was written that Brent appeared to be dependent on his parents and acted as an adolescent. In addition, he had expressed a desire to live independently, yet had no plan for how to accomplish this goal. Furthermore, although Brent began to participate in inpatient group therapy sessions toward the end of his hospitalization, it was recorded that he appeared "spacey" and did not seem to have much cognitive insight. We have frequently observed this same spacey behavior at home; however, at times Brent's conversation suggests tremendous insight, especially when the topic is not about his feelings.

Brent's apparent lack of insight regarding his suicide attempts was and continues to be a prominent concern for Press and me. Brent still has not been able to fully articulate how he was feeling when he cut his arm. He was later able to share with his therapist that the pressure of school had become overwhelming and that he did not know how to handle the stress. Whenever we have attempted to process this incident with him, he has not wanted to talk about it. His mannerisms at these times seem to suggest that he is embarrassed by the incident. I felt it was important to process the incident with him because I was hoping that such a discussion would assist him in recognizing how he had felt prior to using the pocketknife on his arm. In turn, I hoped that if he would be able to identify these feelings, if they should occur in the future, he could tell us about them and receive help before trying to harm himself.

Several months after Brent's hospitalization, I was helping him turn his bed mattress one day and noticed a steak knife stuck between the mattress and box springs. Seeing my surprise, he gave out a nervous laugh and immediately hid it. When I asked about the knife, he said he forgot that it was there. He had put it there around the time of his previous suicide attempts. Again, he did not want to expound on the incident. However, he did assure me that he had no thoughts of suicide and promptly returned the knife to the kitchen.

After Brent returned home from the hospital, he occasionally mentioned something to Press and me that reminded us of his naïvete or lack of worldly knowledge. For example, he asked us how you "get the voices" that one of the patients said she was hearing. She told the counseling group about the voices, and he did not know what she was talking about. It was a relief to hear that Brent never heard voices and did not understand what it meant, especially when the psychiatrist was trying to rule out psychosis. We explained how some people who are diagnosed with a psychosis hear voices, which physicians try to control with medication. We also mentioned that the doctors were not sure at first if he was experiencing a psychosis because he did not share much information. He seemed satisfied with our answer, but we are still not sure how much he understood.

Upon discharge from the hospital the admitting psychiatrist diagnosed Brent with atypical bipolar disorder. Dr. Rubin and Dr. McCartney did not agree with the diagnosis and were disappointed that neurological testing had not been conducted. Dr. Rubin diagnosed Brent with depressive disorder and anxiety disorder not otherwise specified when Brent returned to his office for a followup visit after his hospitalization. He recommended that Brent continue to take the medications prescribed while in the hospital. Brent has kept on taking these medications, with reminders, since then.

Although Brent has never made another suicide attempt and promises that he will not harm himself again, he does experience mood changes that suggest depression and/or anxiety. Lately, I have wondered if these mood changes, persistence with dating and the associated risk-taking behaviors could be due to a comorbid bipolar disorder, as the admitting psychiatrist suggested. In fact, Brent recently told me that he had noticed that his behavior is different from the way it was several years ago and that he does not know why he is unable to control some of his impulses. When he has taken risks and engaged in behaviors that he knows are not good for him, he does not want to stop. It is only after this mood passes that he realizes that he made poor decisions.

Two months ago, Brent, Press, and I shared our concerns about bipolar disorder with Dr. Rubin. As a result of this discussion, Brent's Depakote prescription was adjusted. During the next visit, Seroquel was added. The additional medication has seemed to make a tremendous difference in Brent's mood and has allowed him to sleep throughout the night, which, in turn, has led to better functioning during the day. We are not completely sure if bipolar disorder is an accurate diagnosis; however, we do know that Brent has experienced significant difficulty with anxiety, mood swings, impulsive behavior, depressive symptoms, and more recently high-risk behavior.

When Brent becomes overwhelmed, he tends to withdraw and spend more time in bed. He does not speak much at these times, and instead pulls the blankets up over his head in an attempt to shut out the world. We have tried to reason with him at these times, reminding him that he previously said that when he felt like isolating himself, he might be heading for a crisis. However, this strategy has not proven very effective. Brent seems to need more time before he is ready to discuss and process these events with us. We are trying to be patient and give Brent more wait time before encouraging him to talk. However, when we find him in bed with the blankets over his head when he is otherwise supposed to be at school or meet a similar commitment, we experience a knot in the pit of our stomachs because we start to relive the past crisis episodes. Moreover, it is challenging at these times to remain calm and allow Brent extra wait time to process his thoughts and feelings with us. Fortunately, as time has passed and Brent slowly learns better coping strategies, remaining calm and patient has become easier for Press and me.

We now know that depression and anxiety are common conditions associated with Asperger Syndrome. Several researchers (Ghaziuddin, Weidmer-Mikhail, & Ghaziuddin, 1998; Tantam,

1991) have found that depression was the most common comorbid diagnosis in adolescents and adults. For example, Tantam (1991) noted that depression occurred in 15 percent of adults with Asperger Syndrome. Anxiety disorder, which was frequently associated with depression, reached significant clinical severity in 7 percent of the adults examined. Therefore, it seems imperative to educate people who interact with individuals with Asperger Syndrome to become more aware of behavior changes that might signal an impending crisis. We cannot accept their comments that they are okay, since many times they do not understand their own feelings clearly enough to acknowledge them and express them to others.

Furthermore, it appears prudent that professionals conduct a complete developmental history of individuals who present with psychiatric conditions such as bipolar disorder, obsessive compulsive disorder, depressive disorder, anxiety disorder, or psychosis to determine if these conditions are truly the primary diagnosis or if an undiagnosed pervasive developmental disorder, such as Asperger Syndrome, is the primary diagnosis. Ryan (1992) found that the eccentricities, emotional lability, anxiety, and fixed habits of individuals with Asperger Syndrome can mimic several other mental illnesses. In some cases of Asperger Syndrome where the disorganizing anxiety is a response to stress and is also accompanied by oddness in speech, it can easily be misinterpreted as psychosis. Unfortunately, the developmental history that we provided while Brent was hospitalized did not seem to be taken into consideration. However, at that time the awareness level of Asperger Syndrome as a separate developmental disability was not as widespread as it is now.

Lessons Learned

Adolescents and adults with Asperger Syndrome may not demonstrate the signs and symptoms of depression in the same manner that others without Asperger Syndrome do. Furthermore, some of the features of Asperger Syndrome can mimic other psychiatric conditions, making it difficult to determine the primary diagnosing condition. Conducting a complete developmental history appears to be one of the keys in determining the correct diagnosis. It is imperative that family members and professionals realize that depression is a serious condition that occurs more frequently with individuals with Asperger Syndrome than in the general population. Therefore, we need to be vigilant in looking for signs and symptoms of depression so we can intervene and perhaps prevent a crisis from occurring.

References

Ghaziuddin, M., Weidmer-Mikhail, & Ghaziuddin, N. (1998). Comorbidity of Asperger syndrome: A preliminary report. *Journal of Intellectual Disability Research, 42,* 279-283.

Ryan, R.M. (1992). Treatment resistant chronic mental illness: Is it Asperger's syndrome? *Hospital and Community Psychiatry, 43,* 807-811.

Tantam, D. (1991). Asperger syndrome in adulthood. In U. Frith (Ed.), *Autism and Asperger syndrome* (pp. 147-183). Cambridge, UK: Cambridge University.

chapter ten

Navigating the
Maze of Social Services

Once a child with special needs leaves the public school system and the special education supports provided, he or she is thrust into a more fragmented system of adult services. Since Brent did not have a special education label in high school, the transition planning for adult services that begins at age 14 for special education students did not happen for him. Brent was doing well academically at the time, and we did not realize that he would ever need such supports. Therefore, his initiation into the maze of adult social services was probably more difficult and confusing than it might otherwise have been since we had to make all the initial contacts with the separate agencies. I do not know how many adults with disabilities could navigate this system without a competent case manager and/or dedicated family member to help facilitate the process.

Developmental Disabilities Services

After our disappointing search for confirmation of the diagnosis of Asperger Syndrome through a private psychologist, we contacted our local Regional Center, which is part of our State Division of Developmental Disabilities. We were treated courteously and in a professional manner during the assessment interview. The examining psychologist was very knowledgeable about Asperger Syndrome and confirmed the diagnosis the first day. The rendering of this diagnosis opened up the myriad services that are available to individuals with disabilities and provided Brent with a case manager who would coordinate many of his services. Brent requested a male case manager, and was assigned a dedicated professional who had many years of experience working with individuals with developmental disabilities and their families. Charles was very busy with his large caseload of clients with developmental disabilities and his own counseling practice. However, he accepted Brent as a client, and two months later when he was able to clear his schedule, he devoted considerable time and effort to assisting Brent. Although Charles was not very familiar with Asperger Syndrome, he was willing to learn and to advocate for Brent. The two years that we worked with Charles were invaluable. Charles recognized Brent's strengths and potential and was extremely encouraging and supportive through his person-centered planning approach.

Shortly after Charles began working with Brent, he mentioned that he would like to contact his colleague Jim to provide services for Brent, given Jim's many years' experience working with individuals on the autism spectrum. Among other things, Jim recommended that Brent work with a speech-language pathologist who was reportedly comfortable working with older, higher-functioning individuals. Specifically, it was hoped that she could assist him with social language skills that would help him pick up the subtle cues in conversation that he usually missed as well as work on other social skills issues. Over a month passed before she called, only to tell us that she was no longer taking private clients and should not have been assigned to Brent. She apologized for taking so long to get back to us, indicating that there was a misunderstanding between her and Jim and that we seemed to be in the middle of it. It was also at this time that we realized the professionals were not used to working with individuals on the high-functioning end of the autism spectrum and were not sure how to help Brent overcome his social and communication difficulties.

After explaining to Charles that we thought addressing Brent's social skills deficits should be the focus of his services, he applied for a small grant from our county developmental disabilities organization to fund social skills training. Coincidentally, he was at the office when the committee was meeting to decide who would be awarded grants, and stopped in to listen. When they announced that the grant for Brent was denied, Charles spoke up to explain the importance of social skills training in Brent's life. Although Brent was a high-functioning individual, he needed to learn these skills so he could become independent. He emphasized that the grant funds would be well spent because Brent had the potential to be a productive citizen, but he needed to learn social skills in order to be more independent and successful in the marketplace.

The committee had never funded services for someone with Asperger Syndrome and was concerned that they might be breaking the rules by awarding the grant to someone who did not have a true developmental disability. That is when Charles told them that Asperger Syndrome is a pervasive developmental disability, and described how it was a highly socially disabling condition. He also explained that because individuals like Brent do not look disabled, they are frequently misunderstood and do not get the services they so desperately need. Following Charles' explanation of Asperger Syndrome and Brent's specific needs, the committee ended up awarding the grant money to be used for Brent's social skills training.

Once funding was secured, Charles asked Matthew, a 30-year-old who worked for a mental health facility, to work with Brent on social issues after his regular workday. Brent accepted this social skills plan but did not seem overly enthusiastic to be involved with what appeared to be a paid friend selected for him. Matthew seemed to be very flexible and told us that he did not want to push himself on Brent. Instead, he would take many of his cues from Brent as to what their planned activities would involve. In the meantime, several other professionals were briefly involved in providing support services for Brent. However, they were already overcommitted and could not continue to be involved after the behavior plans and goals were written.

This was becoming very frustrating. One day Brent went to an appointment only to find that the professional had forgotten the meeting. To make matters worse, the person never called to apologize for missing the appointment even after Brent left him a message to ask where he was. Brent – the person with the identified social skills problems – made the perceptive observation that it seemed ironic that the people who agreed to help him with social skills training did not demonstrate courtesy by calling or apologizing to him. Many months passed with promises of phone calls and followup from another professional that did not happen unless Press or I persistently placed reminder phone calls. Again, it made me wonder how persons with developmental disabilities get services without a good case manager and/or involved family members. This makes us particularly grateful for Matthew, who has been the only consistent service provider in Brent's life for the last three years.

At first, Matthew and Brent typically went out to eat or to see a movie. Even though Matthew told Brent repeatedly that if he was ever in a crisis or just wanted to talk, he could call him any time at home or at work, it took over a year before Brent developed a relationship with Matthew and initiated calling him when he had a problem or wanted to do something special. Up until then, Matthew was the one who called Brent each week to see what he wanted to do. Although Brent seemed to look forward to getting together, it apparently did not occur to him that he could call Matthew to share his concerns or even call to set up a meeting. While Brent is now finally initiating more calls to schedule and reschedule activities, he never calls Matthew just to chat.

In fact, Brent refers to Mondays as his "evening with Matthew" and anticipates Matthew's Monday afternoon call to find out what he wants to do during their time together.

Vocational Rehabilitation Services

Several months after Brent was diagnosed with Asperger Syndrome and had been fired from Greg's company, we made an appointment at the Vocational Rehabilitation (VR) office to see if Brent qualified for their services. Brent was assigned a young, enthusiastic and competent counselor who had a master's degree in counseling from the same state university that Brent had attended for two years. After looking at the paperwork we brought her, Kate informed us that Brent qualified for services by virtue of having a documented disability. Since we had provided all the necessary documentation, a considerable amount of time would be saved and services could start right away. Kate asked Brent if he would like to attend a vocational exploration program in a small group at one of the agencies VR contracts with to conduct vocational assessments. She suggested that the satellite branch of this organization might be best because it was not as crowded and busy as the main downtown branch, and therefore presumably less anxiety-provoking for Brent. In addition, the female counselor/team leader there was familiar with Asperger Syndrome. Kate admitted that she was not familiar with this condition, but was willing to learn more and listen to our suggestions so she could assist Brent. We shared with her the main areas of difficulty for Brent, including social skills and communication difficulties, perseverative interests, anxiety, and depression. Brent agreed with her suggestion and was given an appointment to meet with the counselor/team leader of the program two weeks later.

Unfortunately, Brent did not like the counseling and vocational exploration group. Already after the fourth or fifth day, he refused to go, but was vague as to why. When I offered to drive him and speak to the team leader, he still refused. Brent finally shared that he preferred working with male counselors. After repeated calls from his counselor/team leader, he agreed to speak with her and told her that he was not ready for a group setting. She later indicated that she thought Brent might be upset with her because she had suggested that he needed additional educational coursework to pursue the occupations of computer programmer, computer consultant or clergy that he had selected. Her assumption was probably correct, as Brent subsequently responded that he was tired of going to school and that he wanted to pursue an occupation that supplied on-the-job training. After all, he had been called a computer programmer at Greg's company and was learning new skills on the job. He wanted to continue doing similar work without taking formal coursework.

I worried that Brent might be asked to leave the VR program because he did not cooperate with the plan, especially since VR was paying for the services. I shared my concern with Kate, who assured me that he would not be asked to leave the program. After consulting with the counselor/team leader, Kate suggested that Brent might want to work individually with a male counselor/team leader. However, the only place where this could be arranged was at the more congested downtown office. Brent agreed to this option and waited out the several weeks until Tony, the counselor, was available to meet with him.

The vocational assessment indicated that Brent had good organizational and clerical perceptual skills. His reading and math skills were within the postsecondary range, and he evidenced average ability to reason and follow written directions. Further, Brent's computer aptitude and literacy scores were good, but his computer programming scores were below average. As a result, Tony had reservations about Brent pursuing a career in computer programming. Regardless, Brent was convinced that he wanted to work with computers.

While Brent was participating in the career exploration program, he was also answering employment ads in the newspaper on his own. In response to an ad for a government clerical position, he passed the first interview and basic skills test, and received an official job offer. Upon this good news, Kate, Tony, and I met to review Brent's assessment results and discuss a plan to help him at his new job – a job he secured on his own. We decided that Tony would call Brent's supervisor and periodically check to see how Brent was doing. He also offered to come to the work site to help, but Brent wanted to try to work completely on his own without a job coach, as he did not want to stand out as being different. Brent had noted on his government personnel paperwork that he had Asperger Syndrome, but no one at work ever questioned what that meant or how it affected him. Tony shared with Brent's work supervisor that he had difficulty focusing on tasks. Two weeks before Brent was unexpectedly fired, Tony was told by Brent's supervisor that he was doing well despite some difficulty staying focused and on task.

I called Kate when Brent was fired to ask for help on what to do next for him vocationally. We decided to meet with Tony and look into other career exploration possibilities. Tony suggested that Brent work at several of the sites supervised by his organization for a week each to see if he would like that type of work before he applied for a new position. He was allowed to select a maximum of three different sites. He would not receive pay since the positions were considered mini-internships. At his first site, where he dismantled computers, Brent did not like the work or the environment. At his second site, he worked as a mailroom clerk in a hospital. He liked this work because there were a variety of different tasks to do and he got to move around frequently. While he had the opportunity to interact with others, he did not have to do so on a prolonged or sustained basis. This seemed to work well. Brent did not feel apprehensive in these social situations and rather enjoyed them. The only part of this position that he was not fond of was the occasional transporting of patients. In fact, one day he stayed in bed refusing to go. When it was explained to him that a typical mailroom job would not involve patient transport, he asked to spend his last week at the same site. The mailroom staff was not able to accommodate him the third week, but scheduled him to go back on the fourth week. The staff welcomed him and reported that he was one of the best clients they had. Unfortunately, they did not have a paid position available.

During this time, Brent suggested that it might be best if he kept his intense interest in computers as a hobby and considered employment in other areas. We agreed, as we had mixed feelings about him pursuing a computer job because it seemed it would be difficult for him to restrain himself from surfing the Net or signing on to chat rooms if he ever had downtime at work. He could get lost in these activities and would not get his assigned work completed.

Brent explored two other positions, bank teller and travel agent, and also job shadowed as a mailroom clerk at a non-hospital mailroom. The job shadowing experience further reinforced his interest in mailroom and clerical work. After conducting an informational interview with a bank teller, Brent decided that the job was too sedentary for him. Two days before he was scheduled to interview at a travel agency, he called Tony to say that he no longer wanted to pursue this interest because he was afraid that if he spent much time talking with people he would eventually "say something stupid" and get himself in trouble.

Application for Social Security

During the time that Brent was exploring careers and was unemployed, I became concerned about his future and his medical insurance needs. He was unable to continue on his dad's COBRA insurance plan because Greg had claimed that he provided Brent with medical insurance. By the time we realized that Greg was not using the money Brent sent him for his COBRA insurance payment, it was too late for Brent to be accepted on his dad's policy. I made what seemed like endless calls to insurance companies and found out how difficult it was going to be to medically insure Brent.

Since Press and I also began having serious doubts about Brent's ability to work on a steady basis, I contacted the Social Security office near our home to see if they could help us with these issues. They gave Brent an appointment to come to make an application for their services. That was when I found out that Greg had not paid Brent's Social Security taxes because Social Security had no record of Brent working that year. This was significant, because we were told to apply for Social Security Disability, which is based on your previous work history and income. We were also told to apply for Supplemental Security Income (SSI), which is based on financial need. We would be notified of acceptance or rejection of Social Security benefits within 60 to 90 days and were informed that we had a right to appeal the decision if we felt it was unfair.

Press and I had an appointment that week with Dr. McCartney, Brent's private psychologist, to discuss our ongoing concerns about parenting Brent. During this counseling session, Dr. McCartney mentioned that less than a block from his office were a team of lawyers who specialized in Social Security issues, whom it might be prudent to contact. The next morning, Press set up an appointment to meet with their intake coordinator 10 days later. We were instructed to bring the Social Security forms we had received, along with documentation regarding Brent's disability and pertinent medical history.

Press and Brent met with Carla, the intake worker at the lawyers' office, for three hours discussing Brent's disability and how it impacted his daily life, especially his ability to work. I provided research that documented the seriousness of the social impairment associated with Asperger Syndrome, including the relatively poor prognosis of adults with this condition. Carla shared that the lawyers only accepted cases that they believed they could win for their clients – they won 90 percent of the cases. Toward the end of this information-gathering session, Carla left the office for several minutes. When she came back, she announced that the firm would accept Brent's case and send the necessary paperwork to the Social Security Administration. Lawyers can only receive a maximum of 25 percent of any back Social Security benefit payments the client receives. Back benefit payments are based on the time between the date the person is qualified as disabled and the date the application for benefits is formally approved. We did not need to pay any lawyer fees until Brent received official notification that he would be awarded benefits.

Over the next 90 days, we made several phone calls to Carla regarding Social Security questions and the status of Brent's application. She was always prompt in returning our calls and providing us with the requested information. She emphasized that we should not deal directly with the Social Security office during the waiting period – her office would handle all correspondence with their office. She asked us to call her after Brent went to see the doctor Social Security assigned him. This visit was part of the determination process and needed to be completed before a decision could be made regarding Brent's eligibility for benefits.

Brent went to see Dr. England, a psychologist, within six weeks of our initial application for services. Upon receiving the notification of the appointment from the Social Security office, I called Dr. England's office to find out where he was located and to ask if I could accompany Brent. I explained that Brent had been diagnosed with Asperger Syndrome and had difficulty providing background information and personal history. Dr. England agreed that it would be beneficial if I came with Brent.

When we arrived at Dr. England's office, he conveyed that he was glad I had called before Brent's scheduled appointment as it had given him time to do some reading on Asperger Syndrome. He candidly told us that he had not been familiar with this condition before my call and assured us that it was not his job to confirm or reject the diagnosis, but to report Brent's daily functioning and adaptive skills to Social Security so they could determine whether he qualified for benefits. I knew that Dr. England was highly regarded in the psychology community, so I was not worried about his skills or ability to interview Brent. However, I was relieved when he clarified his role in the determination process because it had been unclear to me. As the interview continued, I became more and more impressed with his ability to obtain information from Brent and to understand Brent's strengths and weaknesses. After approximately one hour, Dr. England said that he appreciated Brent's honesty and willingness to share information about himself. He then commented that after researching Asperger Syndrome and meeting Brent he thought that his 42-year-old brother might have undiagnosed Asperger Syndrome. He thought his brother had mannerisms that made him stand out and appear rather odd much more than Brent did.

Again, he complimented Brent on his willingness to share information and asked him if it would be okay to talk with me for a few minutes, to which Brent immediately agreed, as he needed a break. Dr. England thought Brent was probably done talking because he seemed distracted and tired after one hour. As often before, this comment made me wonder if Brent's ability to present himself as subdued, quiet, and controlled was an asset or a liability. It would seem to be a tremendous asset. However, it also caused others to believe that he was functioning better than he truly was. Only when he had major meltdowns or crises did we realize he was struggling.

In the meantime, Brent continued to work with VR. In fact, his compliance with VR was part of the Social Security process. Press and I truly believed that Brent would be able to eventually obtain gainful employment, even if it was on a part-time basis. Our hope was that he would obtain Social Security benefits to help support him until he was able to work, but more important, we wanted him to have medical insurance to fall back on in case he was not able to receive medical insurance coverage through eventual full-time employment. It was beginning to look as though Brent might not be able to handle full-time employment.

I mentioned our concern over these issues to Tony during one of our phone conversations. Vehemently noting that he did not believe that Brent was disabled, he proceeded to state that he had worked for Social Security in the past and would not have given Brent's application for benefits a second look. Hearing this, my stomach was in knots and I became enraged. First of all, it was not Tony's place to make those comments. He was not a doctor who could render diagnoses. Second, I became concerned that the person who was going to look at Brent's application might also assume that Brent did not have a disability and therefore refuse to give his application a closer look. I managed to gather myself enough so I would not appear enraged or defensive, and calmly commented that when Tony saw Brent in his office he was well groomed and appeared just fine. I believe that Tony was used to working with clients who were more cognitively impaired and who also physically appeared to be disabled, whereas Brent did not. Nevertheless, Asperger Syndrome is a highly disabling social disability. The fact that many individuals with this syndrome look so normal makes it easier for others who do not understand the disability to assume that they are lazy or trying to manipulate the social services system.

I also felt that Tony might be suggesting that we were try-ing to take advantage of the system by indicating that Brent was disabled. I understand that the Social Security system is trying to eliminate misuse of their funds, and fully agree they should. However, in no way did we want to take advantage of the system. We were trying to secure benefits that Brent needed and we thought he was rightfully entitled to, given his legitimate disability. I explained to Tony that we did not want Brent to sit at home and vegetate while he collected Social Security checks. We wanted him to work and feel valued as a contributing member of society. We also wanted him to work for paid employment or as a volunteer so he would have something to wake up for each day.

Furthermore, I calmly explained to Tony that he was unaware of most of Brent's history and that, for example, Brent was not getting to his office completely independently. Most mornings he needed to be coaxed to get out of bed even though he had set his alarm. I tried to work at home in the mornings to make sure he left for his scheduled appointments on time. I knew that I would not always have this luxury, but I hoped Brent would eventually be able to function independently as he had done in the past. At the time I did not realize that Brent's behavior may have been telling us that he was not ready for career exploration and that his disability was affecting him even more than we suspected. I was worried that Brent might be dismissed from Tony's program because of noncompliance, which would probably jeopardize his chances of being considered disabled by Social Security. We were caught in a dilemma – by assisting Brent, we were making him appear less disabled to those who did not understand his disability. Brent confided in Charles, his case manager, that he did not think Tony understood him or his disability. Again, I was amazed at Brent's perception, especially since I had not voiced these feelings aloud for Brent to hear.

I continued to tell Tony about Brent's life over the past several years, including his suicide attempts and hospitalization. Gradually, Tony's adamant belief that Brent was not disabled seemed to soften. At the end of our conversation he admitted that if Brent were his son, he would probably also request consideration for Social Security benefits. This exasperating conversation confirmed for me the lack of public awareness concerning Asperger Syndrome. I wondered how Brent was going to be able to maintain employment since most people did not seem to understand the needs of individuals with Asperger Syndrome. In general, people are able to recognize and accept that someone is disabled when he or she looks different or is in a wheelchair. Brent did not look physically disabled, yet he was living with a neurological impairment that affected his social skills, communication skills and his behavior. In other words, it was a pervasive disability that appeared hidden to a casual glance.

Back to Vocational Rehabilitation

Tony initiated a meeting to review Brent's recent career exploration experiences. On the day of the meeting Press and I left our jobs early to attend. Brent was supposed to drive from home to the meeting on his own. Since Charles was working at his office 1.5 miles from our home that day, he offered to check in with Brent to make sure that he was ready to come to the meeting. This precaution reflected the fact that we were never quite sure if Brent was going to follow through on his commitments, which was immensely frustrating.

We did not want to treat Brent like a young child and insist on taking him everywhere he needed to be, because we wanted him to learn responsibility and become independent. However, when he made a commitment and did not follow through, we were torn as to what to do. Did he need more of our assistance or was he overwhelmed and unable to handle things that appeared to be simple and not anxiety-provoking to us? It was hard to know how insistent and firm to be because his current behavior was different from what we observed several years earlier in high school. For example, Brent had kept his commitments and acted responsibly without our assistance.

At any rate, on this particular day, Brent was still in bed when Charles called, so he went to our home and picked him up. He subsequently called us at the meeting to let us know that they would be late. When Brent arrived, he agreed to pursue job placement with a job goal of part-time mailroom clerk. He was assigned to work with an older female job specialist to locate a job.

Again, we had to cajole Brent into keeping his appointment with the job specialist. He told us that what they did was boring and that she did not have any computerized searches. All he did was look at job notices and the newspaper, which he insisted he could do at home. He did not understand why he had to drive so far and hassle with finding a parking spot downtown just to look at the newspaper. He did have a legitimate point!

Social Security Benefits

Three months after Brent applied for Social Security benefits, we were informed that he qualified for both Social Security Disability and Supplemental Security Income (SSI). His disability payments were fairly low since he did not have a long work history. That is, he had been a student most of his life and had worked part-time while in school and essentially full-time only during summers. Brent began receiving SSI payments, but needed to wait five months after the date he applied for his disability benefits to begin. Much later when his income from Greg's company was finally uncovered, we found out that he should have been receiving a higher disability payment. That involved readjustment of his income; besides, he needed to pay back funds to the SSI program because he was no longer eligible for their benefits.

Press and I must have contacted the SSI coordinator several dozen times over the year trying to straighten out Brent's payments. When we realized that he had been overpaid, we wanted it changed right away, as we were concerned that Brent would spend the money and not have it available when the Social Security

Administration requested it be returned. While the coordinator claimed to be happy to work with us because we were so honest and tried to keep abreast of Brent's situation, I suspect our frequent phone calls must have become tiresome for him.

Throughout all this, I kept wondering how individuals who do not have someone to advocate for them manage to navigate through the bureaucratic maze. Two years after Brent began receiving Social Security benefits, I attended a conference on disabilities and learned about a publication that helps simplify some of the Social Security benefits and work incentive training. It helped me to know that others were also struggling to understand the complex Social Security system and that an organization had taken the time to simplify this information. This publication is listed in the references at the end of this chapter and can be obtained by contacting the Montana University Affiliated Rural Institute on Disabilities at (877) 243-2476.

Creative Career Programming

In February of 1999, while Brent was experiencing difficulty working part-time as a cashier, we went back to the meeting table with Tony and Kate. Charles surprised us by also attending. I had specifically not invited him because he had already spent a considerable amount of time helping us, and I knew he was extremely busy. We were very fortunate that he came, because he suggested an innovative idea that would help Brent tremendously. He had just found out that the Regional Center was considered a training site and that Brent could work in an unpaid internship there with the computer staff. The best part of it was that David, the manager, was a former case manager who had worked with Regional Center clients who had developmental disabilities before earning his degree in computers. In fact, David was the one who had suggested this option to Charles. Charles described David as flexible, knowledgeable about disabilities and computers, and an excellent teacher. Brent agreed to try that option to see if he would like to again pursue a career in computers and also learn more about computers in an on-the-job training environment.

At this point we thought it best to have a person-centered planning meeting with the service providers and friends in the community who could help support Brent. After several weeks of planning, scheduling, and rescheduling, we arrived at a date that the key players in Brent's life could agree upon. Jim, who was assigned by Charles to oversee Brent's services, asked his former colleague, Mark, to facilitate the meeting because he had extensive experience with Future's Planning, a form of person-centered planning. On a Friday evening, Brent, Mark, Matthew, Charles, Jim, David, Dr. McCartney, Press, myself, another colleague of Jim and Mark's, and two of Brent's friends met to discuss Brent's future. It was so encouraging to see all of these people gather at our home to problem solve how we could all take a part in helping Brent realize his dreams. Moreover, most of these people were not receiving compensatory time or pay for being there. In addition, Brent's church friends had an opportunity to experience a side of Brent they had not seen before. They knew that Brent had some difficulties but had assumed that he was just shy. They were interested in learning more about his specific disability and how they could be of assistance. When Brent was asked to describe where he envisioned himself five years from that night, he responded that he was not able to envision that far ahead and would like to change that question to where he saw himself in one year. Even that was a challenge for him. Brent experiences difficulty with long-range planning and realizing the consequences of his decisions.

David readily agreed to provide an unpaid internship position at his work site for up to three partial days per week if that was agreeable to Brent. He had two staff members who would probably work with Brent the majority of the time. Brent thought this sounded like a good match and said that he would like to work at the Regional Center several half-days per week. Mark's colleague also knew of a job site that might be able to provide Brent with an unpaid internship and promised to investigate that possibility.

The rest of the meeting was spent trying to devise a plan to monitor and assess the effectiveness of the internship. Jim agreed to write up a behavioral plan and evaluation plan. Jim was a great writer. However, he had written several excellent and detailed plans in the past that had not been successfully monitored. Everyone was busy, and I was afraid that if the internship was not tightly monitored, it would not be successful. Also, we had learned in the past that writing a plan without input from Brent would not produce the best results. Given that Brent tended to keep his thoughts and feelings to himself, we suggested that someone at the work site check with him briefly before he went home each workday to see how his day had gone and if he had any questions or concerns. David was willing to be an active part in the process and to check on Brent and report his progress on a regular basis to the team. However, we had difficulty pinning down who would be David's consistent contact person. I was willing to serve in that role, but we all agreed that it would be best if one of the service providers did so. Charles agreed to begin as the contact person on an every-other-week basis.

Brent began trouble shooting and configuring personal computers during his internship with David. Things seemed to go fairly well. Brent soon found out that work can be fun and interesting and at other times rather mundane and routine. He also learned that sometimes the completion of projects depended on waiting for other people who did not have things ready when they were needed. Brent immediately noticed the difference in the personalities of David's two assistants and commented on this. David said that Brent's perceptions were correct and that picking up on these differences was an important skill in the world of work. Brent was learning which individual it would be best to approach for one type of assistance and which would be better for another. As a result of this experience, our hope was that Brent would be able to discern whether or not he wanted to work with computers as a career, feel that he could contribute as a worker, learn some technical skills and, perhaps most important, learn some of the social skills necessary to maintain a job. Since 90 percent of a person's ability to sustain employment depends on his or her relationships with colleagues and only 10 percent seems to hinge on technical skills, given that Brent's disability involves deficits in social and communication skills, we were much more concerned with the social skills aspect of his internship. Working at a site that serves individuals with developmental disabilities seemed to be the safest, most nurturing place for Brent at the time.

Mark's colleague did not contact us regarding the internship he had mentioned, so we left him several messages to follow up. Finally, Brent started that internship in July after he had worked at the Regional Center for three months. Unfortunately, the supervisor left the company for another job opportunity within two weeks. Brent continued to volunteer there, despite the lack of direction and supervision. Often there were no specific tasks for him to do and he was told he could surf the Internet. Nevertheless, we encouraged Brent to continue volunteering on his assigned day while we contacted Mark's colleague to problem solve the lack of supervision and continuity in the internship.

Meanwhile a rock cracked Brent's windshield while he was driving to the internship site one day, causing him to have to replace it with the money he had in his bank account. He was also issued a parking ticket because he parked in the employee parking area. His volunteering was financially causing him some difficulty. We wanted him to learn responsibility and see his commitment through, so we encouraged him to persevere. However, it was becoming obvious that there was not enough work for him to do and that he might just as well stay home and surf the Net if that was all the position had to offer anyway.

In the meantime, David's department needed some help installing upgraded computers and software, so Brent put more hours in at the Regional Center to assist with this transition. His work was valued, and he appeared to enjoy the recognition he received for his efforts. One day during this time, Brent sent out a network message to the staff saying something like, "Hi. How are you?" When David heard about it, he asked Brent if he had sent it. When Brent said yes, he firmly told him that he did not want him doing anything like that again.

Soon Brent began to stay in bed and refused to go back to the Regional Center. David later told us that while he wanted Brent to know that sending silly messages at work was not appropriate, this behavior did not jeopardize Brent's job. He had been rushing to a meeting the day of the incident and did not have time to fully explain the situation to Brent. Yet he did not want to wait until the next week to speak to Brent about the problem. Brent began sleeping a lot and making excuses why he could not go to work. Once we found out how David felt about the situation, we explained to Brent that his services were still needed and that David was not holding a grudge and was not angry. We wondered if Brent was feeling embarrassed or ashamed and could not face going back to the internship. It took tremendous effort to cajole him to return.

Around this time Brent decided that he would like to pursue a career in computers and return to school to obtain the appropriate credentials. I called VR and set up a meeting so we could discuss this option. VR agreed to pay for Brent's 60-week program at Vatterott College, provided he maintain regular attendance and passing grades. The necessary paperwork was completed in a timely manner and the process went very smoothly.

Medicaid and Medicare

Charles suggested that we allow Brent to apply for Medicaid because it might open up more service options. The Medicaid program is operated by each state and provides medical benefits to individuals with disabilities who qualify financially. We hesitated, because we were afraid that he would lose the good medical care that he was receiving under my medical insurance. After the fiasco with Greg lying about Brent's medical insurance, I was so happy to find out after days of searching for alternate medical coverage that Brent could be added to my medical insurance until he was 25 years of age. We obtained this coverage for him, and he contributed to the cost. However, this coverage was expensive and was becoming a financial burden for Brent. Still, I was relieved that he had medical coverage.

Brent had to wait two years following his first Social Security Disability check before he could be considered eligible for Medicare services. This is the same medical insurance that individuals over 65 years of age are eligible for if they have paid into Medicare while employed. It does not cover reimbursement for most medications though. We decided that we needed to take Charles' advice and find out if Brent was eligible for Medicaid, especially since his insurance payment through my medical insurance was more than he could afford. As a result, Press and Brent went to the local office and completed an application for Medicaid.

Our fears about the medical services Brent could access through Medicaid were unfounded. To our surprise, we found out that the services were quite good. Brent was able to continue seeing his psychiatrist, Dr. Rubin, but he did have to find a new family practice physician because his current physician did not accept Medicaid patients. His psychologist, Dr. McCartney, also did not accept Medicaid, but he did accept Medicare, which pays for 50 percent of psychological services. Brent learned that he was eligible for Medicaid services shortly after he applied since he was already considered disabled through the Social Security Administration and was receiving a low monthly Social Security Disability check.

Once Brent was accepted for Medicare services, his Medicaid coverage became secondary coverage. He uses Medicaid to pay for his medications and to pay the monthly copayment for Medicare as well as other copayments owed to doctors he sees who accept Medicaid. After Brent's disability income was increased, following the uncovering of his employment with Greg, he was no longer eligible for SSI and totally free Medicaid. He was then put on the Medical Assistance Spenddown Program and now needs to reapply for this medical coverage every three months. We have had to remind him to do this and have explained several times that he needs to pick up a renewal application and complete it and then order his prescriptions and ask for a receipt of their cost. Then he needs to bring all this paperwork to his Medicaid counselor so she can approve his Medicaid Spenddown renewal before he is able to pick up his medication for $2 per prescription from the pharmacy. Brent also needs to be able to plan ahead so that he won't run out of medicine while he initiates the process. We have had to assist him every time, although each time he assumes a little more responsibility in the process. We want him to be able to do these things on his own so he can be independent. Considering how complicated and time-consuming all of this is, I wonder if many people miss out on some of their entitled benefits.

Other Adult Concerns

The most recent issues that we have raised with Brent's case manager from the Regional Center include our desire to access individual supported living for Brent as well as possible additional mental health services, because we are concerned that he is also dealing with bipolar disorder. We have been told that the mental health department assumes that the developmental disabilities department provides all the necessary services. We were also told that funding for developmental disabilities is anticipated to be severely cut and that it could be years before Brent will be considered for independent supported living services. We did not apply for these services earlier because we believed that Brent would be able to live independently and probably would not need much supervision. At this point in our Asperger Syndrome roller coaster ride, Brent definitely appears to need more support than any of us had imagined.

Another issue we have had to deal with as parents of an adult child with Asperger Syndrome is the provision of a special needs trust and estate planning. If adult children inherit money or property from their parents' estate upon their death, they might lose government benefits if the inheritance is not protected in a special needs trust. We contacted a lawyer who drafted our wills and the special needs trust. His services were not inexpensive but definitely worth it. Not all lawyers can write these special needs trusts; however, frequently lawyers who specialize in disabilities and the elderly can provide this service.

Unfortunately, when we found out that Brent had Asperger Syndrome, we were not given a handbook of all the services we should investigate and all the future ramifications of this lifelong condition. Such a handbook did not exist. We learned more and more each day by researching and studying the available literature on Asperger Syndrome, going to support group meetings, and attending conferences on autism spectrum disorders. It is my sincere wish that some of what our family uncovered will be helpful to others so that everyone does not have to reinvent the wheel and start accessing this information from scratch. Fortunately, Asperger Syndrome is becoming better known and the public awareness level has increased significantly since we began our solo journey through the social services systems.

Lessons Learned

Navigating the adult social service system is more complicated than the school-age special education system. Many of the services are fragmented, and often the separate systems do not know what other related organizations are doing or how much their services might overlap. Case managers for individuals with developmental disabilities seem to have huge caseloads and cannot always provide individual assistance to help their clients navigate this incredibly complex system. Although many social service programs are federally based, each state operates them a little differently. We live near the border between two states and have learned that the services and delivery systems are very different depending on which side of the state line you reside. This is something that needs to be kept in mind when relocating.

Adult issues to consider include whether or not the individual can maintain steady employment and live on his or her own. Some individuals with Asperger Syndrome live on their own without assistance and some even marry and raise families. If the individual is not able to live alone and maintain employment, Social Security benefits as well as Medicare, Medicaid and even food stamps may be considered. For some families, a special needs trust may be needed to protect the individual with Asperger Syndrome.

In conclusion, our experiences – although not atypical – do not have to be the experiences of others. There have been and continue to be individuals who, despite not having had the benefit of an early diagnosis, have compensated for their difficulties and have led and continue to lead rewarding and fulfilled lives. Again, my hope is that readers will benefit from the lessons we have learned so that they can avoid some of the negative ones and profit from the positive ones. This is such a hopeful time, given the current research efforts and increased knowledge available about Asperger Syndrome that we are fortunate to have today.

References

Shelley, R., Hammis, D., & Katz, M. (2000). *It doesn't take a rocket scientist to understand and use social security work incentives* (4th ed.). Missoula, MT: The Rural Institute Training Department.

PART IV

OTHERS'
PERSPECTIVES

chapter eleven

Living with
Asperger Syndrome
by Brent Barnhill

The Basics

Living with Asperger Syndrome is like a never-ending roller coaster ride. Sometimes I have days when it seems everything is going my way. Other days I am not so with it! Since my life revolves around my computer and winning sweepstakes and contests, I tend to make these interests my priority instead of the basics of daily living such as taking a shower, brushing my teeth, or rising out of bed before 1 p.m. I now get up at 10 a.m. and seem to have better, but not total, control of my sleeping habits.

This may sound odd to you, but I talk to some people on the Internet who are doing the same thing. I talk to several people in the chat rooms who also say they have not taken a shower when it was 4 o'clock in the afternoon. Please note that I do groom myself like any other normal person. I just do it when I need to leave the house. If I am not motivated or simply have no intention to get ready, you may find me looking like I just woke up. The first thing I do every morning before I shower and dress is retrieve the postal mail to see what freebies have arrived.

Responding to Change

Our mind is a powerful piece of machinery. My mind is on a constant motion of logic flowing in and through me just as if I was a computer. If my mind gets overloaded, I tend to shut down and crash just like a computer. If some changes occur that I do not like or are not expected, some alarms go off in my head just like an error message displayed on the computer. If the program is not terminated and dealt with immediately, the whole hard drive may become corrupt. In this case, the hard drive is my mind.

The way to prevent the mind from becoming overloaded is to take precautionary measures. By working in short spurts and taking frequent breaks, I can reduce stress. It is very important to have an environment where everybody is working together to achieve success. Having a co-worker or special disabilities coach to turn to when I am overloaded is a useful tool. However, I have not been able to initiate this on my own in the past. When I am overloading, I tend to act irrational, which leads me to my impulsivities.

Obsessions

When I was a child, I was always the kid who was out of place. I was much of a loner and did not know how to even act towards my peers. The only thing I knew how to do was misbehave to get attention. By the time I finally realized I did not have to misbehave to get attention, I was already in high school. To my surprise, focusing hard on studies helped me a lot through my high school years. On the other hand, my peers were focusing on the future such as girlfriends and boyfriends or even marriage.

During this time, I was obsessed with baseball cards and even the computer. My dad had a Commodore 64 computer until the power supply blew out. I was so into buying and trading baseball cards, and my father had found a friend at his job that was into the same thing. My father bought me factory unsorted Topps baseball cards in bulk for my birthday and other special occasions. I would sort them by hand and have a blast! I must have had over 40,000 baseball cards. I now only have a few old sets and a lot of common cards if anyone is interested.

After high school, I decided to attend Northwest Missouri State University in Maryville, Missouri, because the school was equipped with computer terminals in each dorm room. What a surprise and new life style this would take me into! I would literally sit at the terminal hours on end learning the ins and outs of the computer system, even how to hack into the system. Although nothing illegal was done, I do want to point out that I did joke around on this BBS (bulletin board system) called ISCA in a forum (where you post messages). I was thinking about putting a virus on the school's computers. This led to a brief message from the administrator letting me know my consequences if I did so via e-mail.

I was so into the computer system (mainframes) that I even asked people on ISCA how I could program on the VAX/VMS computer operating system at our school. Yes, I made a few programs here and there since people were willing to help me make little programming job routines. I guess what most fascinated me were the commands and the power I felt when executing them on the computer. I would literally turn on my computer to see if anybody local was on to chat with through this computer command called "finger," which is used widely on UNIX operating systems.

Impulsivities

Besides acting impulsively while on the computer, I have many other incidents that I would like to share with you. One of them is the impulsivity of gambling. It may not seem like a weird disorder, but it is even harder for people with disabilities to conquer. I know that if I let myself (if I had a job now), I could very well go out to the gambling boats and gamble my money away. I think the best thing that has happened to me was the realization that I did have a gambling problem. I took care of this by giving up my ATM card and having a maximum of $20 in my pocket. If I go out with friends or family, I now have a limit. I think that putting limits on how much money you spend and actually doing everything in moderation would benefit people with similar disabilities. I also think that a parent and child must both agree on these limits; it even could extend toward friends as well.

Next, a problem I had was Internet auctions. I would use my bank debit card online and make bids on items I really did not have a need for. For instance, I bid on a networking piece of software, and I did not even have two computers nearby to use. I would see a deal, could not resist it, and would ask for more than one of each item. The final clincher to the auction saga was when I mistakenly made a bid for 22 VCRs on an auction site. My parents were mad at me at first but were glad I told them about it. The company said they would not cancel the bid, so my parents suggested I take all my money out of the ATM machine before it was too late. My mother thought that legally a company could not charge anybody until 72 hours had passed; but I do not know if this is the case. After I did so, she went to the bank with me to switch to an account without a debit card, so that it would make it harder to buy stuff directly online. I need to point out that I am now making wiser decisions. A nice online service called PayPal lets me pay directly from my bank account. I even asked my doctor if there were any medications that would help me control impulsivity because this was troubling me.

Another problem I have is excessive chatting with people on the Internet! It seems like when I start chatting in non-Christian rooms, all other people talk about are sex-related issues. I guess people who are introverts do not know how to relate towards people. This then makes me feel lonely and needy and wanting a female companion. I am often in the Microsoft Service Network (MSN) chat rooms saying, "Any single females care to chat?" and sometimes, to my surprise, I receive no responses. For me, since I have an impulsive personality, chat rooms tend to be a place to find my worth, talk, and meet people online. On the other hand, it makes me feel very needy, so I try to not be in chat rooms for a long period, especially when I see regular chatters there all the time. It is like they have nothing to do with their lives but stay online. I definitely do not want to become like these people. Finally, making a virtual friend is much easier than making a true friend!

How I Relate to Others

Many executives and supervisors, to my knowledge, do not know much about this disorder. Therefore, it is even harder for them to accommodate for this condition since they might not know about it or just do not care to accommodate for people like myself. People with Asperger Syndrome are sometimes viewed as downright lazy and unmotivated. They often think we do not care. However, the truth is that we do care, but just do not always see the importance of serious issues. Luckily, employers are being encouraged to make accommodations to a certain extent. In my opinion, I have yet to see the administration take any such action to help people with this condition.

People often view us as immature because we say childish remarks without thinking of the consequences. Sometimes people think we are cold and calculated, but we are not. I do not know when to socially stop saying remarks. That is why it is good to have a supervisor or boss, or even a co-worker, work alongside that person and cue them when to stop before the damage is done. I can recall an incident (not related to work) that had to do with a girlfriend of mine. I said if she had a better job than working at McDonald's she could pay her bills off. Even though I try to be sensitive towards people, my words sometimes do not display it correctly. I know deep down inside what I want to say, but it just comes out differently. Clearly, I was trying to make a mere suggestion and not be hurtful towards my ex-girlfriend!

Lack of Common Sense

I know we all tend to at some time in our lives need more common sense, but let me tell you my story. When I do not follow my daily routine, missing medication doses, sleeping in, not taking a shower, and being disorganized to the point of missing appointments, I lack common sense. Obviously, one should take a shower and have a regular sleeping pattern. When I miss a dose or two of medicine, my parents tell me I am acting weird. My mother would say I act "sassy." If I miss two doses, I get the shakes and my body reminds me something is not right.

I can definitely recall a time when I actually drove all the way down to St. Louis to "get a woman" in bed. I had never experienced a sexual relationship before this time, but I was obsessed thinking about it. I met a woman on the Internet who agreed to meet me and asked me to page her when I got to the Quick Trip near her house. To my surprise, her husband called the Quick Trip store and told me to go home or he would call the police. I did go back home and never met the woman. As I drove home, I realized in my heart this was wrong, and I needed a change in my life. When I tend to do things lacking in common sense, I know I let my emotions take over my mind.

Even though I love to get freebies off the Internet, I sometimes fill in forms too quickly and it backfires. Recently, I signed up for a free wine tasting and gave the web site my phone number by mistake. Since I do not drink wine, I literally had to pry myself off the phone to just say no. Being assertive and saying no to things I know are not right for me is another thing I have a hard time doing.

We all know that if you do not like something, you do not do it, right? Wrong! Not if it involves women! Sometimes hormones get the best of me as I said before, and I want a girlfriend. This is not just for a physical relationship, but also for companionship. I would attend an event even if I did not like it, if it involved seeing women. Since relating to others in person, especially the opposite sex, is harder for people like myself, I tend to get a little lonely at times and can feel useless, not worthless.

Summary

In conclusion, I know that people like me need multiple supports such as church friends, supportive parents, and possibly professional care. If a piece of the support falls short, others may be in for a rude awakening and not even realize that the person with Asperger Syndrome is having a problem until it is too late to remedy. All of these support pieces need to be in proper alignment, just as the pieces of a puzzle must fit together properly to create the complete puzzle picture. I am reminded of the analogy of the body of Christ in which every body part (referring to each person) has an important role in life and is needed to make the whole body work well, including the person with Asperger Syndrome. It often takes patience to find this role.

Depression, and more seriously suicide attempts, can plague people with Asperger Syndrome who fail to take their medication. Even our closest allies, our parents, may not know our feelings until we tell them how we feel. I urge anyone who has been diagnosed with this syndrome to be open to all avenues of help and care.

chapter twelve

A Father's Perspective
by Press Barnhill

hat is it like to be the father of an adult son with Asperger's (AS)? I have had many and various emotions over the years about my son and his problems. His problems through elementary school seemed to be related to delayed maturity and I thought that time would heal that. His high school years were fairly smooth, with Brent getting good grades and motivated to succeed. He was still very immature for his age and had almost no friends – but he seemed happy and was getting positives out of school. I was frankly optimistic about his future at that point. The diagnosis of AS was still years away, and he had proven he could perform at a high level. Brent even earned membership in the National Honor Society!

For the past few years, Brent has basically behaved like a teenager emotionally (though chronologically he is now 25 years old). Teenagers are not all that much fun to raise and Brent is not an exception. While this chapter may seem overly negative to some, please realize that the last few years have been difficult for me emotionally and have forced me to accept that Brent is always going to be a person with AS. He has behaved poorly in many situations over the last few years. In fact, to me it seems that his behavior has regressed since he left high school. My expectation is that people learn from their mistakes – and Brent has learned sometimes. But with social situations and with job situations, he has repeated the same mistakes. Accepting this has been hard for me. This could be highly related to his teenage emotional state and I am optimistic that he may indeed grow out of this current stage and be able to live on his own and lead a more normal life.

College was a real challenge for the whole family. Brent's school offered free 24-hour Internet access in each dorm room and Brent could not stay away from it. Each semester Brent got more into the Internet and less into his studies, so he failed his classes the last semester he was there. When Brent failed the written English test that was required to pass the English composition course his second semester and again in his last semester, that may have been when I started to give up on Brent maturing into an adult any time soon. How would he be successful if he could not stay away from the Internet and could not pass a basic writing test?

Brent came home from college and moved back home for the foreseeable future. I finished off our basement with a small bedroom, full bath and a recreation room, and Brent moved into his "pad." He now leads a relatively private life from us, as he eats mostly on a different schedule than us, and "works" on his computer many hours each day. He sleeps at least 10-12 hours each day. He still lives in our home and probably will live with us for many years to come. I must confess that I had not expected to have my grown son living with me at age 51!

Time Issues and Change

Having an adult son with Asperger's has led me to gradually change my expectations. My vision at Brent's birth was for a son who would grow up, have a family, a college education and a good job. After his first few years, I was focused on him trying to cope with school on a day-by-day basis. Little time was spent contemplating the future. In high school I had visions of him getting his act together and maybe even graduating from college. His failure in college, his subsequent failure at two jobs, and his diagnosis of Asperger Syndrome at age 21 have changed that. My expectations are now that Brent will need at least five more years living with us to gain maturity and that we will help him through his tough times. We may be supporting him, at least emotionally, for the rest of our lives.

Brent recently finished a 60-week program to be a personal computer technician. We are pretty proud of him but it was a real challenge to help him through it. Almost every time something changed, we had a crisis. The school moved to a new and better location and Brent was very upset that their Internet service was not working. He wrote a nasty e-mail to the school and decided he had to quit. Days and lots of counseling later, he went back and was fine for a while. He got a different teacher who was new to the school, and Brent again wanted to quit. We talked him into continuing the program, but it was close. Change is very hard for Brent.

I am never sure what Brent is thinking or whether he is upset or content. Brent can rarely tell anyone how he feels – and can almost never remember how he felt even a day or so before. He will be upset – and we do not know it until he starts acting out. Then he is frequently too upset to tell us what the problem is. After he has calmed down (maybe a day or two later), we start the 20 questions game. Brent hates to be asked a lot of questions, but he cannot articulate his feelings so we have to work hard to get him to express himself. Even his psychiatrist and his psychologist both have a hard time getting Brent to express his feelings about himself, which can be very frustrating.

When Brent is upset, he can be pretty obnoxious. He has learned the art of sarcasm pretty well – but in an immature way. Once he has a line down that gets a response like "Oh, really?," he uses it over and over. His ability to differentiate when a line is appropriate is very poor. One thing he has learned is that we are pretty tolerant compared to outsiders, so we get a lot of his sarcasm. I must confess that I am frequently sarcastic, too. His sarcasm can get me pretty mad at him, especially when he directs it at my wife. Sometimes he does it just to get a rise out of me, at other times it is as if he does not know what he is doing. The net result is that I can be upset with him and he may or may not know why. Needless to say, this can be very frustrating to all of us. Remember that Brent is now 25 years old – but frequently he behaves like a teenager.

One issue that is hard for me to deal with is separating Brent from his Asperger's. The problems we have with him are numerous, but are frequently related to his syndrome. I do believe he tries hard at times to overcome his disability, but at other times it seems as though he just does not care. How is a parent to know when the AS person is really trying and when he is using his condition to avoid something? When I get mad at him, it is difficult to be mad at the condition and not at the person.

We have frequent issues with doing things on time, at the right time or when we want them to happen. Chores are a constant battle. Brent has only a few things to do such as clean his basement "pad," take out the garbage, and mow the lawn in the good weather. He must be constantly reminded to do these tasks, which then creates a feeling on his part that we are "on his case" too much. Clearly the Asperger's affects his ability to keep track of his responsibilities, but is it his immaturity or is it the Asperger's that causes the conflicts? Or is he just lazy? If it is the Asperger's, then I am guilty of pushing too hard at times. If it is just him, or his laziness, then I may be justified in pushing him. If it is just that he has delayed maturity, then am I asking too much of him? This uncertainty is very frustrating.

Frustration and Money

Easily the strongest emotion I feel in dealing with my son is frustration. Brent is frequently very close to acting almost normal – but you never know when something will throw him off. I feel that he could do so much better if he just tried a little harder and listened to the people who are trying to help him.

Brent sees a psychologist twice a month and weekly meets with a social skills counselor. In addition, he gets some help from his friends at church and, of course, we are always trying to help him. Much of what he hears just never seems to stay with him, or he cannot apply it in his life.

A good example of this frustration is how Brent handles money. When Brent moved back to live with us, he started to be interested in deals on the Internet. Brent had a job with the government for five months that paid a good wage. It was Brent's money and we felt that he could spend it as he chose. Much of it was wasted on a lot of junk that was priced so low on the Internet that Brent had to have it whether he had any use for it or not. For example, he bought two children's computer games for $10 each because they were so cheap. He later sold them at a garage sale for much less than the price he paid. Eventually, we had to take Brent's debit card away from him (with his concurrence) because he could not stop buying things. The final crisis came when he bought 22 VCRs at about $35 each that would have wiped out his entire bank account. We stopped him at that point from buying on the Internet.

ATMs are another problem for Brent. If he needs money, he finds an ATM machine and gets what he needs. Each transaction typically costs an extra $1.50 because he frequently cannot seem to find his own bank. Brent wasted over $40 last year in ATM charges. This was a critical problem when he went on a series of trips to the gambling boats and lost $50 a day over a two-week period. His solution was to cut the card up and throw it out the car window. Now he had no access to his money! Of course, we had to suggest that he apply for a new card.

Brent can be easily led by people (especially girlfriends) to do silly things with money. He had a girlfriend in a town 175 miles east of home, who had no job and massive college debts. She had just flunked out of school and was desperate for a boyfriend. Brent found her on the Internet and spent five months dating her. The travel expenses were high, and he spent money because the only entertainment in her town was going to the local department store. By the time the relationship was over, Brent was just about broke – but he did not know it. Brent has not been able to balance his checkbook. Only because his mom helped him, did we find out that he had spent almost all of his savings on this girlfriend. It was a real surprise to Brent that he suddenly had no money.

The frustrating part about money and Brent is that he doesn't compensate for his weakness with money. Despite a lot of counseling and training, he does not have the sense to keep track of the money he has in his account. We have to constantly keep up with this for him. He is fully capable of using the computer to keep track of his checking account – but he cannot always remember to even record his ATM withdrawals or the checks he writes. Each month is a messy adventure when his mom balances the checkbook. But the worst is not being sure when Brent will go on some buying binge – and not tell us about it. When he keeps his mistakes a secret, it is also very frustrating as we usually find out later when we have to do a lot of damage control. Just recently, however, Brent seems to have been handling his cash and his bank account better. He was able to get his bank account online so he can see has cash position daily, and he has stopped using other bank ATMs as much.

Communication and the Concept of the Future

Attempting to communicate with a person who has AS can be frustrating. If men are from Mars and women are from Venus, then people with AS are from some place like Neptune or Uranus. They can really say some far-out things. A funny example in our family occurred over 15 years ago when Brent got frustrated with his younger sister. A popular saying at the time was "Earth to a person," meaning that the person was acting "out-of-it" or not paying attention to what was going on. We had used the phrase on Brent by saying, "Earth to Brent" to let him know he was not paying attention. Brent did not get it quite right one day and said, "Mars to Kristen," to his sister. Needless to say, it took all of us a while to figure out what he was trying to say.

For most of Brent's school years he was diagnosed with neurological problems. Certainly, we had a lot of trouble getting and keeping Brent's attention. But it goes beyond just getting his attention. Even when he is listening, he may not understand. People with AS do not pick up the nonverbal aspects of communication such as the subtle differences in tone of voice. Both can change the meaning of the words being used. I have a hard time making sure he understands without treating him like a child. It hurts his feelings when I go too hard on him, and sometimes I go too easy and he misunderstands. Patience is a key skill that parents with AS children need. I do not always have patience and I can easily lose it with Brent. My sarcastic comments can be confusing to him.

The future is a very hard thing to communicate to people with AS. They seem to live in the present, and the idea that their current actions could have consequences even a few days from now is hard for them to understand. Long-range thinking is most difficult, as we found out when Brent went to college for two years. When he was in high school the teachers had a tendency to make sure that long-range projects or papers were being worked on. They let us know due dates and helped the students by having outlines due, first drafts due, etc., prior to the final due date. No such help was available to Brent in college, and he had a terrible time planning for term projects and papers. It seems that a few weeks into the future are just about the same as years to individuals with AS.

Perhaps the biggest problem that Brent had in college was managing his day. When he was interested in something like the computer, he could stay up very late into the early morning hours – and then oversleep his mid-morning class. If he did get up in time for the class, he was tired and would need a nap.

Unfortunately, a one-hour nap could end up lasting many hours – and he would miss his afternoon classes. Brent even lost track of time during finals week and overslept a final exam. When Brent was taking evening classes, he overslept them by taking a nap in the afternoon and forgetting to set his alarm. Even now if he sets his alarm, he frequently takes naps with the stereo on and cannot hear the alarm anyway. One day recently Brent's alarm was beeping and he was not getting up. When I asked him why, he said he was having a really good dream and did not want it to end. So he stayed in bed! The consequences of these behaviors on the future seem to be beyond Brent's comprehension.

Brent also has difficulty in determining how long things should take. He cannot accurately calculate how many hours a task will take. If a task takes over a few hours and has to be split up into parts, he is pretty lost. Here is where we have had to help him by giving him structure. We frequently have to make sure he starts a task with enough time to finish it, and we have to break down larger tasks into smaller parts. A good example is cleaning his downstairs pad. It could easily take many hours to really clean his bedroom, his bathroom and the recreation room. We set up a schedule for each part of the larger task and spread it out over two or three days. We limit his Internet time during this period so he knows that it has to be done.

Remembering about appointments is particularly difficult. Last week Brent only had three appointments all week since he is now finished with his computer technology program. A doctor's office called him to move an appointment, but Brent did not write it down or remember the call. He scheduled two of his three appointments at exactly the same time. Luckily, when the doctor's office called to confirm, I answered the phone and was able to reschedule one of the appointments. We have tried to have Brent use an appointment calendar – but he cannot remember to use it or to bring it with him when he leaves the house. Brent has a lot of problems with time.

Concentration on a Task

Brent has a lot of problems staying focused on a task unless it is his special interest, the computer. He frequently waits until he has no clean clothes before starting a wash. Most of the time he will start the wash, but completely forget about it until the next day when he needs clean clothes – they are clean all right but soaking wet because he forgot to put them into the dryer! Three out of four weeks we end up putting his clothes into the dryer for him (sometimes because we need to do a wash ourselves). There have been a number of times when Brent did the same thing at college and forgot about his clothes in the basement of the dorm for days. More recently, I had to hand wash some clothes and dry them quickly so he had something to wear to an appointment.

Motivation is the key to concentration for Brent, as it is for all of us. However, when there is only one real interest, it is hard for a parent to use it to motivate their child. Luckily, Brent's interest is in computers and the Internet – and a lot of things can be related to this interest. If his interest were in trains or coins or trees, we would have a lot more difficulty using them to motivate him. We can partially control the amount of time he spends on the Internet, as it is our phone line he is using. We long ago got a second phone line primarily for Internet access and faxes. The Internet is such a good source of information that he can pursue his interest and also accomplish important tasks. I realize that this is not true for many families because their child's interest is too narrow.

Perpetual Teenager

Perhaps the most long-range concern I have as a father is that Brent is so delayed in his emotional maturity. When Brent was first diagnosed with AS at age 21, the psychologist indicated that she thought Brent was about age 12 emotionally. It is now over four years later and Brent still acts like a young teenager. Unfortunately, this young teen is in a 25-year-old body. Brent has had a number of very bad relationships with women who used him and took advantage of his extreme interest in sex. Emotionally, Brent cannot handle "twenty something" women, but his interest in women is intense. Too many times to count we have counseled Brent, and had others counsel him, on appropriate behavior – but to little effect. He is not yet capable of overcoming his desires and impulsivity – a potent combination that seems to dominate his behavior.

This Sunday morning Brent woke up late for church. He did not go to his Bible study class, but did make it to church. He claimed not to be feeling well, but he did go to church anyway. This is unusual for Brent because when he doesn't feel well, he just stays home. He wanted to do some playing on the Internet first and did not have time to shower. Instead he decided to just use a lot of deodorant and brush his teeth. When church was over, he came home to brush his teeth again and improve his appearance because a girl he likes showed up at church and the young single adults decided to get together for lunch and an informal party. All of a sudden he feels fine and rushes home and back out to meet the group and this girl. This is classic behavior for a young teenager!

Another aspect of his emotional state is his poor tolerance for authority and his feeling of being controlled. Like any teenager, he wants to have control of his time and his activities and does not want dad telling him what to do. This has been going on for years and may continue for many years to come. One professional indicated that he believed that AS people may have an emotional maturity of about two-thirds of their chronological age. That would put Brent at a maturity of about 18. I believe that is about where Brent is emotionally, based on his behavior.

How long is any family supposed to have to deal with a teenager? I have a serious worry that Brent will be acting as a teenager for at least five more years. That is a real challenge to me as a parent. When we had children, my life plan was to be an "empty nester" about four years ago. To have the flexibility to travel, to relocate to new parts of the country, to be able to do some serious charity work and maybe missionary work was my goal for the end of the century. Little of that is possible now. My plans must be delayed many years and maybe indefinitely. It is very hard not to feel resentful at times.

On the positive side, I have learned a lot in dealing with Brent. I am more patient than I was as a younger man. I realize with clear conviction the power of words to hurt others and to help others. I have learned to realize that Brent could be much lower functioning and we could be burdened much more. My heart goes out to those we meet with children who have more serious disabilities.

Impact on the Family

We were blessed with a second child born a little less than three years after Brent. She is now married and living in Chicago with a wonderful Christian husband. However, she suffered because of the time we spent with Brent. Brent was such a burden on us that there is little doubt that our daughter was deprived of some of the nurturing and quality time that she wanted and probably needed. I was working full-time and was not as good a father as I should have been. At that time I thought that Brent would just grow out of this immaturity. I was in denial that he had a real and permanent problem.

Through age seven our daughter was apparently a happy, contented child who had friends and was doing well in school. Preschool was a breeze for her compared to the difficulties Brent had. After age seven she started to gain some weight, and lost much of her pleasant attitude. I believe she was starting to resent the parent time that Brent was taking from her and was starting to be embarrassed by his inappropriate behavior. Brent preceded her in school and was at times in the same school as she was. Brent had by this time gotten a pretty powerful reputation as a problem child and our daughter suffered as a result.

My wife was very good at trying to bring friends into the lives of both of our children. Brent could not do well with friends as he could not relate to their interests, was socially inappropriate, and easily overwhelmed by others. Our daughter seemed to go into a bit of a shell with friends. She basically ended up with just one friend at a time and that frequently was a competitive relationship. She excelled at school and got a lot of pleasure and positive reinforcement for doing so well. She also took up a musical instrument and did reasonably well.

Our daughter tried many different things as a preteen. She tried twirling, dancing, Girl Scouts, ice skating, swimming, and soccer, just to name a few. Each activity was done for a year or so and then dropped. I feel now that she was searching for a way to find herself and to get our attention. We did try, as I was an assistant soccer coach and my wife constantly was taking her to practices and events. We went to games and to shows. However, it seems that nothing she did or we could do would make her happy. I believe her resentment about time and her embarrassment about her brother was a lot to overcome.

Having a special needs child in the family puts a special strain on the marriage. There is less time for each other, the frustrations frequently are spilled out on the spouse, and the strain can spoil intimacy. I am told that statistically marriages with a special needs child are much more prone to divorce. Certainly there is every reason to believe it based on our experience. Divorce just makes it much worse for the parent left caring for the child. That is a burden I do not see how any one person can bear. Fortunately, my wife and I have been married 28 years and together we have gotten through the many challenges.

One of the biggest problems is when one of us (usually me) gets mad at Brent and acts to punish him or express anger at him for what he has done or not done. The other spouse sometimes sees the situation from a less invested position and comes to the defense of Brent. This then has the effect of redirecting the anger to each other instead of at Brent. Good for Brent, not so good for the marriage relationship! This has happened many times and has led to many emotional outbursts on both of our parts.

Lucky for us, we are frequently in different emotional states so that when one of us is completely exasperated with Brent, the other can step in and calm the waters. The problems are magnified when we are both emotionally spent or over-invested in the particular problem. As we are both in challenging jobs, our emotional states sometimes are not very complementary.

We recently took our first two-week vacation alone together in our marriage. We never had family or friends who we felt could handle Brent for a long period of time. This last time Brent spent the first week with relatives and the second week home by himself. Unfortunately, he made some bad choices while he was alone – so our fears have been rekindled. Not being able to get away from a special needs child is a special source of strain for a marriage. Even as a small child, Brent was too much for relatives and friends to handle for an extended time. Generally we were able to get away for a few weekends each year and that helped. However, for anything longer than a weekend, we always had that nagging worry of what was happening back home. It has now been 25 years and that same feeling is still there.

We make an effort to go away by ourselves at least four to five times each year for a weekend. Sometimes Brent will go on a trip with his Bible study class and we will get some free time alone. Most important for our marriage is the time we take to go out on dates together or to go dancing. We started square dancing a few years ago and still go out two to three times each month. We also attend a lot of local theater and an occasional movie. Eating out is a favorite activity for both of us, as is playing golf and taking a 30- to 40-minute walk when the weather is good. We make a conscious effort to talk about our issues and have a pretty strong marriage. We participate in the marriage mentors program at our church and currently mentor two couples.

Lessons Learned

In summary, I have learned a lot from Brent. Perhaps the greatest lesson I have learned is humility. I have some pride in my abilities and have been generally successful in life. With Brent, there is little day-to-day sense of success or accomplishment. Frequently things are three steps forward and two or three steps back. I have had to learn many lessons I did not want to face. I truly feel that God has placed Brent with us to let us know that we cannot be successful without His help. Developing a daily prayer time is a major change in my life. Without the challenges of raising Brent, I might be far behind in my spiritual development.

I have had to learn to encourage Brent even when I did not want to. This has helped me with others, as I have learned to be an encourager at work and in our church programs. There is great satisfaction in helping others. Encouragement is a key activity that helps almost everyone. I think I am a better manager and a better person for what I have learned from interacting with Brent.

Brent has certainly led us to learn about people with disabilities. Without Brent, I would be ignorant of most of the types of disabilities, of the programs that can help people like Brent, and of the problems in securing services for individuals with disabilities. Our experience in taking Brent through his school years and all the problems we had with obtaining his diagnosis have helped us to assist others facing the same ordeals. I am a better person by being the father of Brent.

chapter thirteen

Comments from Other Parents and Family Members

nsights from 41 relatives of adolescents and adults diagnosed with Asperger Syndrome follow. Their experiences and perspectives provide priceless understanding into their lives and give us a glimpse of how this syndrome has affected them and their family member with this condition. First, Brent's maternal grandmother briefly recalls her memories. Forty anonymous contributors follow with their thoughts.

Brent is my first-born grandchild, born in 1976 in Ohio. His grandfather and I first visited him when he was 10 days old. I understood his birth was a traumatic one, but when I first saw him, I saw a sweet baby boy with big, blue eyes.

One of my recollections that something seemed different about Brent was when he was a toddler. He and his parents were visiting us in Florida. Brent wanted something in the refrigerator. He didn't say a word to me, but took my hand and lead me to the refrigerator and put my hand on the door handle. I opened the door and Brent proceeded to point to what he wanted. During the entire time, he did not say a word but just kept looking at me with a look in his eyes I can only describe as "help me." He used no vocal communication.

The other incident that stands out in my mind was when Brent was visiting us again when he was four years old and had a toilet accident in our pool. While he was being scolded verbally, again the look in his eyes said innocently, "What's all the fuss about?" Brent spoke volumes with his eyes, and it seemed that he just didn't think what he had done was a problem.

As the years went on, I know his parents were periodically having him checked both physically and emotionally. However, no correct diagnosis was made until February of 1998 when he was diagnosed with Asperger Syndrome.

Comments from 25-year-old Brent's maternal grandmother

I think the most difficult challenge in living with an individual with Asperger Syndrome (AS) is learning not to take comments and behaviors personally. Much of the frustration a person with AS feels vents itself as anger or hostility toward those around him or her. At the same time, those on the receiving end are also the ones expected to have the most understanding and patience. The only way to achieve this understanding and patience is to try and maintain your perspective and separate the individual with AS from his or her behavior … and that is usually easier said than done.

One of the more interesting aspects of living with an AS individual is both their predictability (for both positive and negative situations) and their capacity to evolve. I do believe that despite many behaviors that are difficult for a neurotypical person to understand, the person with Asperger's really wants to "fit in" and try to be accepted. Probably their greatest frustration is that the so-called "normal" world doesn't appreciate the depth and breadth of challenges they face every day and how hard they do try. I often think that someone on the autistic spectrum has to work two or three times as hard to grow, cope, or otherwise get through life. I admire the stamina they seem to possess.

Appreciation of those challenges also brings me to another point, the obsessions or special interests that are all-consuming that come hand-in-hand with Asperger's. These fixations or interests are a lot easier to accept if you understand that they are a point of security and creativity for an individual with Asperger's. Looking at them from this perspective makes the thousands of trains or fixation with dinosaurs, or whatever, more interesting for the "normal" person.

I guess the point of my comments is that, like with anything else, perspective makes all the difference in the world. If we look at Asperger's as a disability or a continuing source of problems or oddities, then we'll never see the fine qualities it evokes. If we look at it from the "glass half-full" perspective, we can more readily accept the inevitable problems and move on to higher ground.

Comments from the mother of a 12-1/2-year-old son

For some parents the hardest thing to hear is that their child has a disability. All dreams and ambitions for that child seem lost. As a mother of four children with autism, two of whom have Asperger Syndrome, I can say that these children are still, and more so, a blessing. When you realize that this is still my child, the same child I had before the diagnosis was given, the child I love, then you can start to see the true love and beauty of what God intended for you to see.

Comments from the mother of two children with Asperger Syndrome, ages 12-1/2 and 15

Today I feel tired, tired of all the struggles with school. Tired of last-minute phone calls from teachers telling me what major project my son hasn't completed one day before the end of the grading period. Tired of the constant stress of trying to keep up with assignments, homework, and the dreaded long-term projects. Tired of the stress homework and late assignments cause everyone in our family. I am tired of constantly having to ask teachers to provide the accommodations in the IEP. Tired of judgmental comments from those who can't or won't understand the real issues. Tired of trying to fix our child's stress with Tums, Prevacid, and Zoloft. I am tired today. I am not tired every day ... today I am "bone tired," "moving-day" tired, "take a day off from work" tired. It is a lonely feeling, but there is always tomorrow.

Comments from the mother of a 13-year-old son

Life with B. has been like a roller coaster ride. Sometimes he does so well and shows so much awareness that I think we really have a handle on things. Other times, he will say or do something so off the wall that I just want to cry a river. I ask myself how he will ever be able to live a happy life with some level of independence. Yet, he's smart and resilient. The roller coaster keeps going. A psychologist once told my husband and I that a way to think of B.'s Asperger Syndrome is that B. is just wired differently. For some reason, that perspective has really helped me. B. is not defective; he just experiences the world differently than most people.

Comments from the mother of a 13-year-old son

It is so hard to express my comments and feelings regarding having a son with Asperger's. There have been many positives and rewards, as well as many negatives and concerns. It definitely affected my previous marriage. My ex-husband never accepted that he did not have a "normal" son. To this date, he feels that there are no problems with C. and that I make too much of his shortcomings and do not focus enough on his positive attributes. He couldn't be more wrong! I treat my son just like his two sisters and expect many of the same responsibilities of him and accountability; but I am also very realistic. C. has many fine attributes, but I know he has many limitations. I worry about what the future will bring. Where will he be in 10 years? And yet, I look back on the past and would never have dreamed we would be where we are today. Such progress and hope!

The comprehension and social aspects will always be a struggle. I worry – will he ever have a "normal" life? And really, what is a "normal" life? And I wonder what will my life be like? Will this impact my future and future relationships? And then I feel guilty for feeling that way. The bottom line is I love my son so much and I wish the very best for him.

Comments from the mother of a 13-year-old son

I am a grandmother of recently diagnosed young man (age 13) who over the years has been punished, ridiculed, diagnosed as ADHD, and medicated to "psychotic episodes" (per a social worker who finally was concerned enough to really look for something other than easy answers). While I know we have a long way to go and that there will be many pitfalls to overcome, it is such a relief to at least know what we are dealing with. I welcome the diagnosis. I realize this syndrome is difficult to accept, permanent as it is, but how much worse to try to deal with the unknown and realize that nothing is working! At least now we can consult other families and learn what works for them and what doesn't. Also, we can read what those in the field are learning and apply those techniques! Most of all, how wonderful to know it isn't our fault and neither is the kid a hopelessly defiant brat, but rather just as baffled as we are about life and all its unwritten rules. Things are still difficult and I have to relearn responses to my grandson. For instance, I am still trying to learn not to reason him into changing his mind, which can be firmly set in concrete within a nano second.

Comments from a grandmother of a 13-year-old grandson

After I was told that my son had Asperger Syndrome (AS), it answered a lot of questions regarding the multiple disabilities that he was facing. Even though he is the one who has AS, it affected and still affects the whole family. We only focus on what needs to be done day by day. We have to adapt to his needs, so my son will always have a positive outlook on his life while he lives with AS. The hardest part of my son having AS is educating the schools, so they know what we need to do to keep him a good student. My son said that the only form of his disability is others being stupid about not everyone being alike.

Comments from the mother of a 13-year-old son

The following is actually a statement made by our 14-year-old son, who has lived with our niece as a same-age sibling since they were both 3 years old. On our way home from a family birthday dinner, which had gone well, some communication difficulties ensued. Our son said to our niece, "Trying to talk to you is like talking to a stranger who does not want to talk to you." When I questioned him later, he said he almost never feels any sense of connection with her or any sense that they are making a connection. The only time he could name that he felt a connection was when they built with Legos™ together. I think this lack of a shared context makes it very hard to feel that one has a relationship with her. I will say that at 14 she seems to be a bit more aware of social settings, contexts for conversation, etc., but it's a very slow process.

Comments from an aunt, who for the last 10 years has been the "mom" of a 14-year-old niece with Asperger Syndrome

---

My son is 14, almost 15, as he so often reminds me. E. was born with medical problems that led to surgery and the need for oxygen. For the first few years, he struggled to heal and breathe on his own. By age 3, he was physically healthy, but we knew there were delays in his mental and emotional development.

For years, we attributed E.'s delays mentally and socially to his birth trauma. At age 12, E. went through intensive evaluations at our local children's hospital. As his mother, I knew we had never gotten the correct or full diagnosis for his condition. He was diagnosed with Asperger Syndrome (AS) along with another rare syndrome, Simpson-Golabi-Behmel. For once, all the criteria for a condition actually fit our son! It was an emotional time as we let go of the past and looked into the future. We knew that his life would always be a challenge for all of us.

We have been fortunate to have lived in an excellent school district that provides well for children with special needs. With a para-educator by his side, E. is able to be included in regular classrooms. We're hopeful that soon his academics will yield to vocational technical training so that he can begin to prepare for life after high school.

As a teenager with AS, E.'s biggest problem is his lack of social skills. When we're in public, we can be sure he will make conversation with friends and strangers, but never know whether what he says will be appropriate. We are in search of social skills classes but have been unsuccessful in finding one locally so far.

The best advice I could give younger parents is to become knowledgeable about AS and be very active in your child's preparation to attend school. It may require hours of research and extra meetings to educate the teachers involved, but your foundation of advocacy at an early learning level will pay off greatly in the end. No one knows your child like you do, so remember that the professionals mean well but can't know your child as well as you do.

Comments from the mother of a 14-year-old son

Sometimes I think it would be easier to take my refrigerator places than to take my son. It's hard to get him ready and to the car. It's hard to get him out of the car and into the store or other destination. Then he won't leave when I am ready.

Comments from the father of a 14-year-old son

My son is my career. I am trained professionally as a registered nurse, but my son is the focus of my life. I plan my job, activities, marriage ... everything ... by first asking myself, "How will this affect our son?" I have been told I am overanxious, and I am, but I don't know any other way to parent a kid with Asperger Syndrome. I adore my son and will do everything in my power to help him be the best he can become. There are the bad days, when I don't think he will ever be able to make it in this world. BUT there are the days of unimaginable joy. When he does something no one ever thought he could do, or when I find out he really has been listening to us and demonstrates a new skill, and best of all, when he does something that I know is hard for him and he does it, I feel on top of the world!

We adopted him when he was three weeks old, and I was the proudest mother ever! I took him everywhere, and if I didn't have him with me, I had pictures to show off. Now he is 14 years old, and he doesn't like to be looked at. He won't shake hands or speak to others unless he feels comfortable. What a complete change! He has forced me to grow in ways I never thought possible. Do I always like it? No. Sometimes, only on the very bad days, I dream of buying him a ONE-WAY ticket back to his country of birth. He has forced me to become a better person, a better nurse, a better spouse, become more assertive, and most of all become an educator. I educate others all the time about autism – my family, my co-workers, friends, and my son's teachers.

I think it is easier for me to have an "adopted" child with a disability than if he was my biological son. I once had a colleague who was in the process of adoption. She was worried about the child having damage from drugs or other damage from lack of prenatal care. I jokingly told her (my son was one year old at the time and seemingly normal) if our child turned out well I would credit his environment, but if he turned out poorly, I would blame genetics. Many years later, I think it is easier for me to not have to give a moment's thought to genetics or something I did while pregnant that could have caused the Asperger's. Please note that I don't think any biological parents cause autism, I just know so many biological parents who take on the guilt anyway. I HATE it when well-meaning people tell me my son's problem is related to his adoption and separation from his birth mother or "He just needs a sibling." For just a moment I take on the "adoption" and "only child" guilt, but then I realize they don't have a clue about our life.

Loneliness is a big problem for me. Other parents are very busy with their kid's activities, and they make new friends with other parents. Our son is rarely involved in activities and tends to make friends with one child at a time. Invariably my son will choose a friend from some of the most dysfunctional families. It never fails if I meet another parent that I enjoy getting together with, our son won't like their kid. I meet other parents at support groups, but it would be nice to have friends that have a kid my son's age that goes to his school.

Comments from the mother of a 14-year-old son

I am a single parent of a son who has Asperger Syndrome (AS). The AS affects him to such a degree that he is considered disabled. After four years of working with the public school system, I realized their methods were failing. The resulting stress to us was overwhelming, so I decided to home school. I gave up my career (I worked for years to become a registered nurse) and lost all income except for his Supplemental Social Security Income (SSI) of approximately $500 per month. It has been surprising to me that higher benefits would be given to the head of household if he or she was the disabled one. As the full-time caregiver and educator of a disabled child, I am unable to work just as if I was disabled myself. Our lives will always be difficult because of this disorder but could be easier if we were not living in poverty.

Comments from the mother of a 14-year-old son

Maybe my son is a flower with five petals instead of six. So what!

Comments from the father of a 14-year-old son

My son J. is currently a 14-year-old eighth grader with Asperger Syndrome (AS). J. has always been a challenge to us. We knew early on that he was going to be a challenge. He was speech/language impaired, extremely hyperactive, and behaviorally difficult. He got into trouble by throwing things, getting into the cabinets, and throwing temper tantrums as a young child. As an older child, he made threatening remarks, was suspended from school, and still to this day does not comprehend responsibility, commitment, and consequences. We care for him and love him, but we are very concerned about his future, his independence, his sense of right from wrong, and his ability to fit into society.

Comments from the mother of a 14-year-old son

Living with T. is a lot like ice skating … fast, thrilling, chilling, scary, fun … We never know if the ice is thin or thick. We cry and laugh. Sometimes the ice cracks; we back up fast; we tire but then go forward. We are exhausted and exhilarated. T. makes us see life and its nuances in a whole different way. He points out many sights and sounds that we would otherwise never notice and enriches our lives in this way. At every stage of development of your child with Asperger Syndrome (AS), you go through a mourning process. In front of you, on the surface, is the sight of the child that "might have been." It is the child all strangers assume you have. But the behaviors dispel the image. You are sharply reminded that the child that "might have been" is not. Much as we deeply love our child with AS, the pain and sorrow never really go away.

T. has incited in me depths of emotion I never believed I had, both positive and negative. He has made me sob with happiness, fear, and sorrow many times in the last 15 years. One of the biggest challenges in raising a child with AS is that our home is NEVER a completely calm place. Over time this takes a toll on parents and siblings – even our pets have learned to scatter when T. is on a tirade.

Comments from the mother of a 15-year-old son

It has been a long and tedious journey for my family through this ordeal. I am considered one of the lucky ones. My son is learning to cope with this mysterious disorder. He interacts with his friends. He tries to compete in sports. He attempts to enjoy life as he sees it. My family is learning to cope with Asperger's Disorder one day at a time. Throughout the trials and tribulations we have faced, we have persevered.

When people first glance at this statement, a question will come to mind of what is this about and why would someone start a story this way? I opted to start my story at the end rather than the beginning. As a parent raising a child with Asperger's Disorder, I often experience conversations about this disorder that are similar to what is written above. Similar in the sense that there are many people who really do not understand what Asperger's is and how it affects not only the individual afflicted with this life-long illness, but the person's family as well.

When J., the second of three children, was born, I automatically checked to see if he had all of his fingers and his toes. I checked his reflexes and eye movement and thought to myself, "He's okay." Little did I realize that there was much more to J. that any motherly exam could ever find. During his early childhood years, I noticed peculiarities in J.'s development; he did not begin speaking in full sentences until 3, he did not start using the bathroom on his own until he was 4, and he had some difficulty with motor coordination. I took J. to the pediatrician and was reassured that he was okay and that he was developing at his own pace and that I should not worry. It was this advice that I took, and we went on. I put all my trust into this pediatrician. I have to confess I was naïve to say the least.

J.'s problems got worse as he entered elementary school. It was so difficult for him to interact socially with his peers. "Difficult" really does not describe the problems this child faced all alone. He was terrified of the world around him. No one was able to understand his thoughts and feelings as his family did. We were his only source of companionship, of protection from the unknown. I made several attempts to find out what was wrong with J. I was given terminology that only a psychologist can understand. He was initially diagnosed with autism, ADHD, and childhood schizophrenia. It became so chaotic for me as a mother. I thought that his suffering was my fault. I felt guilty because I was unable to help him through his anguish, his torment. These feelings that were inside of me first started as a hindrance, but soon I was able to use those same feelings to create change. I didn't accept what was told to me about my child. I decided to seek help from an outside source. Answers to many of my questions finally came through J. being diagnosed with Asperger's Disorder when he was 7 years old. Upon learning about the disorder, I realized how it all fit. This enlightenment was my catalyst to do more for those in a similar predicament. I began studying psychology. My son's struggles became my motivators for change. Change for my son's daily functioning; change for the field of psychology; change for others afflicted with this disorder; change for my peace of mind.

I can write a book on my child's story, so can the many individuals that deal with this disorder on a daily basis. What I want to convey the most is that the only way to help someone with Asperger's Disorder to live comfortably with this lifelong ailment is to be aware and share that information with everyone. I can say thankfully that because of knowing more about this old, but mysterious disorder, J. is working toward coping with situations we take for granted as being easy. J. has exceeded my wildest expectations. His will to take charge of his life gives me a renewed sense of determination. As I said at the beginning, we were one of the lucky ones.

Comments from the mother of a 15-year-old son

_____

It does not matter how much you explain. Co-workers, relatives, friends, church members, even doctors really DO NOT UNDERSTAND the effect on a family and the demands placed on a family who has a child with Asperger Syndrome. There is a sense of aloneness for the Asperger Syndrome family that is never quite overcome. Confusion, setbacks, progress, successes, tears.

My son is 15 years old now and is doing well. But it has finally soaked in that this journey called Asperger Syndrome never ends. All my life I am planning and striving to help him. It is a very long journey.

Comments from the father of a 15-year-old son

Life with my Asperger's son is somewhat like riding a roller coaster. You never really know what's around the bend, especially if your eyes are shut. However, if your eyes are open, you can see many things that lie ahead. You learn to prepare. It becomes second nature. You learn to talk openly to others who are involved. We knew there was something special/different about our son from the time he was a few months old. We were given an ADD diagnosis at 5 years of age, but we knew there was more. Yes, he had many ear infections. It often took two to three different medications to clear up. He also had two sets of tubes. Finally, after years of different doctors and psychiatrists, social skills therapy, etc., they told us when he was 11 that he had Asperger Syndrome (AS). Since then, it has been confirmed many times. We've always been very active, his advocates all his life. I remember one IEP meeting when he was in the sixth grade. It was a very important one. No one was looking forward to it, and there were 14 of us in attendance. Beforehand I made a trip to Dairy Queen. I brought a variety of Blizzards to the IEP meeting. It broke the ice and they all still talk about it. The old adage that you can catch more bees with honey is true! Doing special things for the teachers is important, especially all the little things.

As we are living through the teen years, the quick turns and ups and downs on our roller coaster have become steeper and sharper. Some days I have great conversations with our son, and he seems to actually "get life." Then something hits the switch and he gets silly, immature, or inappropriate again. Inside my head I look at him and say, "Who are you and what have you done with my son?" Then I silently sigh and think, "I guess they did give him the right diagnosis after all."

For the most part, our family of five revolves around our AS son. He's funny, demanding, challenging, and we love him! He has helped to strengthen my faith. It's funny … it hasn't been until the last five years or so that I have been a little more daring regarding real roller coaster rides. I never liked them before, but now I find them more tolerable. Maybe that's because I've been on so many of them now, so to speak, in my daily life. We never know what the day ahead will hold. All I know is that we'll always be riding a roller coaster with him. No matter when and what, there'll always be constant advocating on our behalf. Have faith in God, and keep smiling. You might as well enjoy the ride.

Comments from the mother of a 15-year-old son

I think we have found a possible solution for our son this year. He is taking courses he loves and attends about three-quarters of a school day. I pick him up at 12:45 p.m. every day and he goes to bed for the evening about 2 p.m. He wakes up at 3 a.m. and showers, eats, and gets ready for school. He has no homework and can play with his new friends on the weekends. I know this is an odd schedule, but I have never seen him more calm or happy. I do miss seeing him in the evenings though, and he doesn't eat dinner with the family. Although we try to wake him per his directions, he is dead to the world. I have to give a lot of credit to his counselor for helping us out. After seven counselors, we found one that really works. If I could share anything, it is that parents need to change counselor if he or she does not work out. This is one of the best things we have done!

Comments from the mother of a 15-year-old son

We need to develop an educational model to address social skills development. The literal interpretation of figures of speech gives these kids much trouble. If one could somehow help them fit in socially, half of the war could be won.

Comments from the father of a 15-year-old son

Asperger Syndrome (AS) can be a frustrating and rewarding disability to live with. Just when everything is clipping along well, something will set him off, and the entire house is turned upside down until he gets it out of his system. On the positive side, he is a very gifted artist and is starting to receive a lot of recognition. Hopefully, he can work in a field where he does not have a lot of human contact.

Comments from the mother of a 15-year-old son

He is very creative, but also very temperamental. There are days that, if he doesn't get what he expects or things don't go how they should go, he can make life difficult around the house and say things he doesn't really mean. But he is constantly trying to be normal and to get others to accept him as that, and I think that is the root of his stress and anger.

Comments from the older brother of a 15-year-old boy

When my son wakes up in the morning and when he comes home from school, I never know what's coming home to me. I never know what's walking in the door on that day.

Comments from the mother of a 15-year-old son

Our main concern is if there will be a place for our son in the real world. Will he find a job, a home, and an independent life? His social skills are the most lacking.

Comments from the mother of a 16-year-old son

My son is 16. He was diagnosed with Asperger Syndrome (AS) when he was 13. His elementary school years went pretty well, but I worked closely with the teachers and spent many hours with him on homework every night. He was diagnosed with ADHD in kindergarten. Things changed drastically when he went into junior high with six teachers and six class periods a day instead of one teacher and 30 students in a class. The school had 900 students all coming and going at the same time! He couldn't cope and spiraled into depression. He was diagnosed with obsessive compulsive disorder in seventh grade. After two unsuccessful suicide attempts, he was diagnosed with bipolar disorder and hospitalized.

Although we thought the hospital would help, it didn't. He was overmedicated and started hallucinating. Then they added more medication. I reacted by removing him from that hospital and moving him to another one. His new doctor recognized the AS and took him off all medication and started over from scratch. We thank God for this new doctor. I don't think any other doctors in our town knew anything about AS at all. Our son is doing very well now. He still has occasional meltdowns when he is overanxious about a change or responsibility in his life. We are so happy that he has made it through those so very difficult junior high years!! He is now a junior in high school, and I have no doubt he will graduate – and with a fairly high G.P.A. Then onward to college, maybe?

M. is a very intelligent and sensitive 16-year-old. His obsession is any and all electronics, especially computers. This is a wonderful strength; however, it can also be an area of struggle as it is difficult to get him off the computer to do other activities. He has explained to us that he would much rather interact with a computer than with a person because he always knows what the computer will do. He can't figure out what a person will do at any given time. Social activities are difficult for him, and if at all possible he will avoid them. He is hyperverbal and wants to talk with people but does not understand reciprocal conversations, so often people are put off by his run-on, very one-sided conversation.

Our biggest struggles are change and transition. Typically a meltdown will happen before he can accept a change. I can usually see these things coming, but sometimes I am caught off guard. These are very difficult and extreme. I sometimes have to hold him until he calms down. This also has quite an effect on my marriage and family life. My husband has a very difficult time understanding the emotional trauma M. is experiencing. He wants to just discipline him and shape him up. It is difficult for him to relate to his son. M. has very few friends, although he has a friendly personality. His doctor states that he will probably go through puberty emotionally in his mid-twenties, and then he will be more "normal." He has made wonderful progress in his 16th year, and I see a promising future for him in computer technology. He'll just succeed in his own way, not ours.

Comments from the mother of a 16-year-old son

Living with my son is always a mystery. You never know from one minute to the next what he is thinking. We could be talking about one thing or be in a certain place and he will bring up something totally different that maybe occurred days or weeks ago. People don't understand him. He looks and appears his age, but may act very immature at times and at other times very mature with his conversations.

My biggest fear is what will happen as he gets older. He wants to leave home and go away to college, but still depends on mom for making decisions and managing his life. He would be the perfect person for people to take advantage of or to influence to do the wrong thing. If he then got into trouble, making him understand what and why he was in trouble could be extremely difficult.

Comments from the mother of a 17-year-old son

We have a sweet 17-year-old girl who has always had behavior patterns that were inappropriate for her age. As she has always been academically advanced, we felt she was just strange – at times rude by being so exacting and precise, and also rebellious by being unable to fulfill simple requests. We were constantly pushing her to conform and not act immaturely. This has only made her strangeness appear a lot worse and her episodes more pronounced.

Knowing about Asperger Syndrome has given us hope for her future. We are now dealing with her differently, which has lessened the pressure on her and allowed her to feel much more relaxed with herself. Using the various behavior modification methods we have learned about through articles and talking with others has made our lives and hers more productive. Now we are working with her and not causing her to be unable to respond appropriately. As she learns her limitations, the episodes are decreasing and she is able to move past some of her obsessive behaviors and realize how to deal with some of her problems productively.

We are now trying to get the diagnosis changed to Asperger Syndrome and wish we had discovered the symptoms of Asperger Syndrome earlier. With a diagnosis at an earlier age, we could have worked with her more productively for a longer time, which would have caused her not to go through a lot of frustration and negative thoughts that came from our handling things as if she was normal.

Comments from the guardian of 17-year-old girl

When our son was diagnosed with Asperger Syndrome at the age of 9, it was somewhat of a relief to us because we had been frustrated for years knowing something was different about him from other children. He was our youngest of four children. We knew nothing about autism or Asperger Syndrome, so we started cramming our brains with information. We attended every seminar we heard about, read books, found an excellent doctor, went to the library, and found a good support group on autism to help us.

We were doing fairly well until he began going through puberty. His doctor put him on medication, which helped a lot, but the hormonal changes caused very frequent, violent, uncontrollable episodes. During this time, I began to have very serious health problems along with one of my daughters, so we had to make a very hard but important decision. We placed our son in an excellent group home run by a couple we knew. This decision was the hardest but best thing we could have done.

Five years have passed and our son is a different young man. He is doing wonderful. He comes home every weekend, and we are very involved in his life. He attends a regular public school and gets along well with his peers and adults. He is very active in our church youth group, has several close friends, loves computers, and is very happy, full of joy and content with his life.

We know our son has come this far because of lots of support, prayer, and the Lord Jesus in our lives and his.

Comments from the mother of a 17-year-old son

Having a child with Asperger's is like living on a roller coaster. The moods change up to down within a second. Our son seemed to be so close to being "normal" at times that I assumed he would reach adulthood and be okay with a little guidance, patience, and support. I am slowly realizing that this is not going to go away and that there will always be problems. The everyday experiences that M. encounters such as doing laundry, getting a job, and banking are very frustrating for him and when a problem occurs, he cannot see a solution. He still does not bathe, brush his teeth, comb his hair, or wear clean clothes without being told to do so. I feel like I am still dealing with a 3-year-old who is 6 foot 7 inches tall! I am always thinking, "He should know better!" When will I wake up?!?

M. is as sweet and gentle as he can be, but has torn our household apart. While he was living at home, my husband, children, and I were always at each other's throats due to the constant conflict that M. caused. The best course of action we ever took was placing him in a hospital at age 17 and requesting that they needed to find placement for him. He could not come back home, or our whole family would fall apart. It was extremely painful for me as a mother, the nurturer, to turn my son away. My husband insisted that this was for the best, and I knew deep down inside that he was right. M. was placed in a group home. He was not very happy, but we were not living on pins and needles anymore, and we could relax and have fun at home. Now that he is in an independent living situation, we have a great relationship with him, and when there is conflict we can go home to our house and be removed from the situation. M.'s siblings also have a better relationship with him now.

As an adult, M. let his hair grow, got a tattoo, smoked cigarettes, chewed tobacco, wrote bad checks, and got fired from a job! Just when we think he couldn't do anything else, he finds something! I know this is what his life will be like, but I still have difficulty accepting it. I want him to be okay and be a functioning adult. We tried very hard to make this happen.

M. is a joy to us, makes us laugh a lot, but is a continual mystery. We just take one day at a time, jump over (or stumble over) the hurdles, and prepare for the next one. It is very important that we stay in touch with Asperger's groups. These are the only people who know and understand what we go through. We are not alone in our struggle. We need to reach out to others and to assist them and listen when we can.

Comments from the mother of an 18-year-old son

At age 9, my dreams for my son died. But at age 18, they have been reborn. Years of hard work have resulted in #2 rank in a senior class of 380+, a full academic ride to a college with an Honors Scholarship (Bright Flight Scholarship) from the state of Missouri, Honors college admittance, and 33 on his first and only try on the ACT. Yes, he is still autistic, but he has many strengths with all his weaknesses. Children with Asperger's can be successful with help from a good support system.

Comments from the mother of an 18-year-old son

Sometimes it is hard to live with our brother. His behaviors are embarrassing and strange. It has made us all very sensitive to people with disabilities.

Comments from the brothers and sisters of an 18-year-old brother

---

I would like to warn all parents of special children to take care of their relationship with each other. You will be hounded to "do something about your child" daily, but no one will call you on the phone or send a note home to remind you to spend quiet time with your spouse or other children. Having a special needs child means you need to have the strongest relationship possible. These children can tear your marriage and family apart if you don't "work" on holding it together. Our children are very special and can bless us deeply. However, raising them in a world that doesn't understand their problem is like living on a roller coaster 24 hours a day seven days a week. Every parent I have talked to with a special child has been told their child's problems are caused by "you," the parent. Teachers, other parents of quote "normal" children, and the general public will all take their turn at telling you just what you are doing, or have done wrong. This seems to be the most devastating. Don't people understand that we love our children dearly? If we didn't love them, we surely wouldn't endure all it takes to get through life with them. In my particular case our child is my husband's and my only child. Still we were told we didn't spend enough time with him; later we were told we spent too much time with him. Just know you can never do things right in other people's eyes. Only God knows what pain we suffer, what hurt we bear every day. Just the heartache of watching your child struggle through daily activities is enough for anyone to bear and we also have to put up with the ignorance of the outside world. The school system was sheer cruelty for our child, but by law we had to send him.

He is functioning at a stable level right now, so life is calm. He is out on his own and isn't causing any problems for anyone. We have researched and investigated every lead we could find. Don't expect someone else to do this work for you. The agencies out there are supposed to do that sort of thing for you, but they don't, or can't. The good people get burnt out fast and the not-so-good people stay forever in their job. You are your own best friend and the only true advocate for your child. I do hate to paint a grim picture for you, but I have found my best hope and strength in the Lord. He always listens, and he doesn't rip you down like the world can. Just do the best you can, but remember to take care of yourself and other family members, because without all of you your child may have no one.

I recommend that you get a guardian or someone else who can pick up the pieces when you are too tired to help or just need a break. Never be, or feel, that you are the only one who can help your child. You need that support system. You are not superparents, and don't try to be. Get help. Look and keep looking until you have a backup. Adult children can be independent and they have a right to that independence. Just keep looking and asking questions. Check out every avenue. And, take care of yourself. I didn't do a very good job of taking care of myself and my family. My son made it, but my family is still struggling to recover. God bless and be with you all.

Comments from the mother of a 20-year-old son

The first thought that comes to mind is the song from "The Sound of Music" about the main character, Maria. Remember, "How do you solve a problem like Maria? How do you hold a moonbeam in your hand?" That is the way I feel about P. In many ways P. is an enigma. Just when you think you have him figured out, he does a 360-degree turn. For example, when P. was younger, the items or subjects he would obsess on would change every few months. P. never slept very long or sometimes not at all (if were trying new medications). We would go through periods when we had to deal with his "fits of rage" at home and school. He was always "the victim." That changed for the most part when we placed him in a private, parochial school. However, he still had to deal with kids who could be unkind or cruel. (That kind of behavior was not tolerated in the private school.) We also went through a period of trying different medications that caused him bad side effects and/or tics. Those were the times my husband and I thought we would pull our hair out!

Having a special needs child created many challenges for our family, not the least of which was trying to explain to our older son, J., who is three years older than P., why we didn't discipline his younger brother in the same manner as we did him. At this point in time, I still go through periods of feeling sadness and guilt that my two sons will never be able to share the emotional bond that most brothers do. I also sense in J.'s comments, from time to time, the frustration and disappointment he feels at having a brother like P. And yet, at the same time, he loves and feels very protective of P. My oldest son is married now with two young children of his own and has begun inviting P. over to their home occasionally for dinner and Nintendo games, which is one activity that he and his brother have always loved to engage in.

My husband, K., and I have had our moments as well. For the longest time, my husband couldn't accept the fact that something was "wrong" with P. People who don't have a special needs child have no comprehension of the tension that is created in a home with a child like P. Sadly, I have heard of many failed marriages due to one or both spouses being unable to handle the stress of their child's disability. It takes an enormous amount of emotional energy and commitment to live with someone like my son. I think our strong faith and commitment to God has been the "tie that binds us." We decided years ago that we were in this thing together, no matter what. I didn't push my husband on the issue of P. because I realized that we all have to deal with "grief" and the acceptance of the inevitable in our own way. One day K. said that admitting something was wrong with his son was comparable to admitting something was wrong with him, that he had somehow failed in not having a perfect child. Up until that moment, I never realized how differently mothers and fathers view their children. It is still difficult for him to deal with P., and I think he feels sorrow at not being able to have the same strong emotional bond with him that he has with our oldest son.

P. will be 21 soon, and I wonder what will become of him once his father and I pass from this life. He has the desire and, I think, the ability to live on his own eventually. But at this point in time, I'm not sure. We have created a living trust to provide for him and his older brother. But what will happen to him should something happen to J.? These are not easy questions to think about and we certainly can't plan for every eventuality. We can only hope and pray that what we've taught him will carry him and serve him well through the rest of his life.

Comments from the mother of a 20-year-old son

Asperger's is just subtle enough that it lures you in – giving you hope. Maybe, just maybe, things will work out okay. But they don't work out.

M.'s perception of reality is so different that when I hear him talk about his childhood, I swear we must have lived in two different houses.

Comments from the mother of a 22-year-old son

Our son's life is very incongruent. He can handle complex items, but not single items. He can handle technology, but has trouble with relationships. We can't get him to wash his clothes. But he took one look at the ceiling fan I was struggling to install, chuckled at my effort, changed a wire connection, and got it to work!

I recently went into his room and discovered that he had built a computer from parts out of six computers he found in the trash. Next to it was a bowl of cereal with dried-up milk that had obviously been siting there for days, since the fruit flies were trying to carry it away!

He can switch in a matter of minutes from a boy of about 8 years old running upstairs yelling, "Mommy, mommy, look at this," to a 22-year-old that is yelling and swearing, so filled with anger that I am afraid to leave my wife and daughter with him alone.

Comments from the father of a 22-year-old son

You no sooner get over one hurdle and there is another. Will my 27-year-old son ever be an independent productive adult? It is so frustrating living with a young adult with Asperger Syndrome. Our son seems to be clueless about the day-to-day activities most people do without thinking. Our son seems to be in a tunnel most of the time, seeing only what is in front of him (usually the computer).

Comments from the mother of a 27-year-old son

It's like I have grown up with a stranger.

Comments from the sister of a 27-year-old brother

My son is 28 years old and has just been diagnosed with Asperger's Syndrome (AS) – it has been a long journey. Early diagnosis suggested learning disabilities, so primary education was at a private day school for youngsters unlikely to be mainstreamed into the local public schools. Small classes in a nurturing environment seemed to work well, although he seemed to have more "personality" issues than academic challenges. He was always on the perimeter of activities and never had close friends. He spent much of his time thinking about and studying weather. It was his consuming passion. For high school he went off to boarding school where it was hoped he could make some friends and achieve academic success that would help determine the next step for him. It was a great success. He had friends and did so well in his coursework that he got into the college of his choice. College was an academic success but a social disaster. He made no real friends at all.

After graduation, he returned home, took a warehouse job, and never was able to develop a social life or jump start a career. I was his best friend. Years were going by. One night I was doing computer work with the television on in the background. Prime Time was doing a segment on AS. When the symptoms of Asperger's Syndrome were outlined, I stopped what I was doing and grabbed a pen to jot down notes. They were describing my son! From there I went to web pages to learn more about AS and tried to find others who have dealt with the condition. I was lucky enough to get an e-mail from Gena Barnhill, who provided numerous resources and support. She told me to contact the Dept. of Rehabilitation to see if they would work with my son. Because the documentation on my son was so old, the rehab. counselor was sympathetic but felt the documentation was too old to verify. So we agreed to have my son go through testing by the state. His primary diagnosis now is Asperger's Syndrome. Interestingly, the testing showed no evidence of a learning disability. He has completed a battery of vocational tests and is working with his counselors on career and work options. He has a new lease on life, and we finally have an understanding of this condition and new options to help him find his place in the community.

Comments from the mother of a 28-year-old son

I spoke to Gena after my son was diagnosed as an adult with Asperger Syndrome. I told her that it was very painful dealing with my son's lack of empathy. I described this lack of empathy as being similar to a pond frozen on the top. I now see a lot of improvement since my son has been on medication and would like to share this information.

After being diagnosed two years ago with Asperger Syndrome, my son now smiles often, occasionally laughs, kids me about my frailties, asks me where I've been if I am late, and tells me he was worried about me. He has an acquaintance. He is on SSI and receives a small monthly amount. He is not yet able to work independently but works well with me here at the farm. I leave a list at least three days a week of things he needs to do. He is able to water livestock, contact neighbors for moving hay, pick up feed, bring in wood, and keep the stove going in winter. He has many uncanny abilities that I no longer try to figure out. He can drive a vehicle and maintains an old pickup truck and a car ... well, reasonably maintains them. His father and brother help some here. He has had very few traffic violations in his driving career and only one or two fender benders.

He cannot tolerate TV and prefers I leave it off. I watch a lot of TV when I am in the house. At least I like to have it on for the news, etc. He is a chain smoker, and this cuts heavily into his income and causes some problems in the house. However, he is good about any rules I make regarding his smoking. He cannot smoke at night ... after I go to bed is "night." Some days if he smokes much, it overpowers the air cleaner machine and he has to take it outside.

He is remarkably responsible about taking his medication and meeting his appointments with the doctor for renewals. I never have to remind him. He handles all this by himself. Once in a while there is a glitch, but not often. He has had several panic attacks but thinks that it was the Paxil. He met with his doctor and they took him off Paxil for a while. He is now on Risperdal, Depakote and periodically, Paxil.

He sleeps too much and lies around too much. I know if I could think up enough stimulating things for him to do he would benefit from it, but I am just not able to keep up the momentum. He is unable to initiate action at the social level. He is lonesome and wants to interact and do exciting things. I regret that I cannot provide these things for him, but I cannot always do it. I did send him by bus to visit his sister in Michigan this past summer. She was so happy and OVERJOYED at the improvement in him and was glad to have him visit. He managed very well changing buses several times and being on the road for more than 20 hours, etc.

He needs young people and female companionship. He is able to articulate his regret that he has no wife and family like most young men his age. His sexual orientation is heterosexual and girls find him attractive. Of course, I think he is beautiful. When he was younger he had more contact with girls but was always incredibly responsible in this matter. He has left behind no children and thinks of the need for them in only the most abstract of terms.

Comments from the mother of a 34-year-old son

My brother was always an embarrassment to me. I think having a better understanding of his condition has really helped. He can only focus on one thing at a time and seems to be more anxious or stressed if you ask him to do too much. He does the same thing on specific days at the same time every week.

Comments from the sister of a 56-year-old man

Final Thoughts

As I conclude this book, I am sitting in a lodge at the Grand Canyon with Press, escaping from our busy life for just three days. We try to take some mini-vacations or overnight get-aways several times a year to regroup and reenergize our marriage relationship. This also helps us to parent Brent better and gives us time to stand back and reevaluate our roles in his life. Our desire is for him to become an independent and fulfilled adult. This was also our goal for our typically developing child. But independence probably will look different for Brent. Currently, we are focusing our efforts on encouraging Brent as he successfully works five hours per week at his new job. We are hopeful that in the near future he will be able to handle the 10 hours per week that his current organization might offer him. We are learning to be patient and celebrate the successes rather than focus on what he cannot do.

Press and Brent will begin visiting the independent supported living homes and apartments in our area to determine if any of these situations might be suitable for him. If they find an appropriate place, Brent will need to apply and, if accepted, he will be put on a waiting list. No one knows how long this will take. We do know that he cannot even be placed on the independent supported living list through our state department of developmental disabilities until Press turns 55. Unfortunately, there are reportedly several hundred individuals already on this waiting list.

Despite the challenges that we have faced and continue to face with Brent, we know that we are not alone in our efforts. Parenting Brent has strengthened our spiritual life and has helped us focus on what is truly important. Much of what Press and I used to value is not really that important in the scheme of life. For instance, Press and I are first-born children and as a result tend to be competitive, perfectionistic, and ambitious educationally. Brent's academic struggles have taught us that being a high academic achiever is not the only admirable pursuit in this life. God has a plan for all of us. He certainly has a plan for Brent, but it is not the plan Press and I had expected. We don't even know what that plan is, but are working on daily trusting God to provide the support we need. Our life path now is different than we had imagined it would be. Most parents of normally developing children had no idea either what their lives were going to be like after they became parents. However, they were fortunate to have some guidebooks on parenting to navigate through life. Most parents of children with Asperger Syndrome have no guidebooks or roadmaps to navigate the uncharted waters.

It is my hope that with the increased awareness of Asperger Syndrome, families will not need to continue to navigate uncharted waters. Support groups for individuals with Asperger Syndrome and support groups for family members can help bring people together and provide much-needed encouragement and assistance. Press and I have started such a group for family members of individuals with an autism spectrum disorder (ASD) for the purpose of sharing concerns and struggles and for disseminating information on ASD and interventions and strategies to help these individuals and their families.

My recommendation to parents of children with Asperger Syndrome is to learn as much as you can about this disability. Some helpful organizations, resources, and web sites are included in Chapter Fourteen. Remember that you are your child's number one advocate and your insight regarding your child's strengths and weaknesses is invaluable to the professionals your child will encounter. We also need to be able to teach others who will educate, play, and work with our children at home, in school, and in the community about Asperger Syndrome and how to interact and support individuals who have this disability. Remember that all parents make mistakes and inadvertently reinforce some of their children's negative behaviors; however, no matter how you parented your child, you did not cause his or her Asperger Syndrome.

Enjoy your children and appreciate their unique characteristics and idiosyncrasies. Brent's sense of humor and naïvete can be so enchanting and refreshing. He has helped me learn to appreciate and value individual differences. The world would be a dull place if everyone had the same beliefs and behaved the way I do. The world needs people such as our children, individuals who are not afraid to dream and be creative. Brent has taught me to appreciate some of the small things in life that I would otherwise have missed in the hustle and bustle of everyday life.

Perhaps all of this can best be summed up by the comments from an 18-year-old man with Asperger Syndrome who wrote:

Between life and death every person is faced with the question of why we are placed upon the earth. After careful thought, I have decided that I am a necessary piece of the puzzle.

When I was born, I was like a puzzle piece, fresh out of the box and now I am trying to sort out the pieces into a pile of matching pieces, which in life is my place where I belong. Once I sort the pieces into piles, I can then assemble these piles into smaller pictures of my life's future. Since I am only 18 years old now, the unfinished puzzle has only been started; but some of the pieces are beginning to fit together. Part of the visible picture is me working as an adult in the world, learning to be self-supportive.

Another larger section of the puzzle is my school life, which is coming together quite nicely. When I graduate in May, I will be ready to join other pieces of the puzzle of society, and I will be able to begin another section of the puzzle as soon as I am an adult worker.

I see myself as an incomplete puzzle, but I think I will be a successful person later on in life. In the end, I will help all society by working in a management position of the store where I am presently employed.

PART V

RESOURCES

chapter fourteen

There Is Help

Organizations

Asperger Syndrome Coalition of the United States (ASC-U.S.)
P. O. Box 351268
Jacksonville Beach, FL 32235-1268
Tel: (866)-4-ASPRGR
www.asperger.org

ASC-U.S. is a national non-profit organization committed to supplying the most up-to-date and comprehensive information on Asperger Syndrome and other related conditions.

AutFriends Inc.
P. O. Box 263
Burlington, VT 05402-0263
Tel: (802)-660-3185
http://afi.autistics.org

AutFriends (AFI) is a non-profit organization dedicated to providing services for individuals with autism, with a special emphasis on serving higher-functioning adults. A majority of the board of directors must be persons on the autism spectrum.

Autism Society of America (ASA)
7910 Woodmont Avenue, Suite 300
Bethesda, MD 20814-3067
Tel: (800)-3-AUTISM
(301)-657-0881
Fax: (301)-657-0869
www.autism-society.org

The mission of ASA is to promote lifelong access and opportunities for individuals on the autism spectrum and their families to be fully included participating members of their communities through advocacy, public awareness, education, and research related to autism.

Geneva Centre for Autism
250 Davisville Avenue, Suite 200
Toronto, Ontario
Canada M4S 1H2
Tel: (416)-332-7877
Fax: (416)-322-5894
www.autism.net

The mission of the Geneva Centre is to empower individuals with autism and other related disorders, and their families, to fully participate in their communities.

More Advanced Individuals with Autism, Asperger's Syndrome and Pervasive Developmental Disorder (MAAP)
Maap Services, Inc.
P. O. Box 254
Crown Point, IN 46308
Tel: (219)-662-1311
Fax: (219)-662-0638
www.maapservices.org

Maap Services, Inc. is a non-profit organization dedicated to supplying information and advice to families of more advanced persons with autism, Asperger Syndrome, and pervasive developmental disorder (PDD).

The National Autistic Society (NAS)
393 City Road
London, EC1V 1NG UK
Tel: +44-0-20-7833-2299
Fax: +44-0-20-7833-9666
www.nas.org.uk

The mission of NAS is to champion the rights and interests of all individuals with autism and to ensure that they and their families receive quality services appropriate to their needs.

Web Sites

Asperger Syndrome Partners and Individuals, Resources, Encouragement & Support (ASPIRES)
www.justgathertogether.com/aspires.html
Online list serv:
http://www.feat.org/scripts/wa.exe?SUBED1=aspires&A=1

Online Asperger Syndrome Information and Support (OASIS)
www.aspergersyndrome.org

Oops Wrong Planet! Syndrome
www.isn.net/~jypsy

Tony Attwood's web site
www.tonyattwood.com

Web site developed by Stephen Shore
www.autismAsperger.info

Web site developed by Liane Holliday Willey
www.aspie.com

Autismconnect is a worldwide, interactive personalized forum for sharing of information by people whose lives are touched by autism.
www.autismconnect.org
Autism/Asperger's On the Same Page
http://amug.org/~a203/table_contents.html

AUTISM Independent UK
www.autismuk.com

R. Kaan Ozbayrak, M.D.
www.aspergers.com

Information on Asperger Syndrome
www.wpi.edu/~trek/aspergers.html

Information on Asperger Syndrome and Chat Rooms
www.aspergerssupport.net

Spectrum
Provides information, news, interviews, articles, chat rooms, and radio.
www.autism-spectrum.com

University Students with Autism and Asperger's Syndrome
www.users.dircon.co.uk/~cns/index.html

Yale Child Study Center Developmental Disabilities Clinic and Research Home Page
http://info.med.yale.edu/chldstdy/autism/page10.html

Autism/Asperger Syndrome Publications

Autism/Asperger's Digest Magazine
Published bimonthly by Future Horizons Inc.
721 W. Abram Street
Arlington, TX 76013
Tel: (817)-277-0727
(800)-489-0727
Fax: (817)-277-2270
www.autismdigest.com

"The Face of Asperger Syndrome"
Special Issue of Intervention in School and Clinic
May 2001 (Volume 36, No. 5)
Can be ordered for $15 from
PRO-ED
8700 Shoal Creek Boulevard
Austin, TX 78757-6897
(512)-451-3246
(800)-897-3202
www.proedinc.com

The Advocate
Published quarterly by the Autism Society of America (ASA)
7910 Woodmont Avenue, Suite 300
Bethesda, MD 20814-3067
Tel: (800)-3-AUTISM
(301)-657-0881
Fax: (301)-657-0869
www.autism-society.org

The Morning News
Published quarterly, Carol Gray, Editor
Jenison Public Schools
2140 Bauer Road
Jenison, MI 49428
Tel: (616)-457-8955
Fax: (616)-457-8442
www.TheGrayCenter.org

Autism/Asperger Syndrome Professional Journals

Autism
*Published quarterly by SAGE Publications in association with the
National Autistic Society*
www.sagepub.com
SAGE Publications Ltd.
6 Bonhill Street
London EC2A 4PU UK
Tel: +44 (0) 20 7374 0645
Fax: +44 (0) 20 7374 8741
SAGE Publications Ltd.
P. O. Box 5096
Thousand Oaks, CA 91359

Focus on Autism and Other Developmental Disabilities
Published quarterly by PRO-ED, Inc.
8700 Shoal Creek Boulevard
Austin, TX 78757
Tel: (512)-451-3246
(800)-897-3202
www.proedinc.com

Journal of Autism and Developmental Disorders
Published bimonthly by Kluwer Academic/Plenum Publishers
233 Spring Street
New York, NY 10013-1578
Tel: (212)-620-8000
Fax: (212)-463-0742
www.wkap.nl

Autism/Asperger Syndrome Newsletters

access EXPRESS
Published by Project ACCESS
Southwest Missouri State University
901 South International Avenue
Springfield, MO 65804-0088
Tel: (417)-836-6755
(866)-481-3841
Fax: (417)-836-4118

Aspects
Published quarterly by the Asperger Syndrome Education Support Network, Inc. (ASPEN™)
9 Aspen Circle
Edison, NJ 08820
Tel: (732)-321-0881
Fax: (732)-744-1622
www.AspenNJ.org
aspenorg@aol.com

Autism Research Review International
Published quarterly by the Autism Research Institute
4182 Adams Avenue
San Diego, CA 92116
Tel: (619)-281-7165
Fax: (619)-563-6840
www.autism.com/ari

FEAT (Families for Early Autism Treatment)
Daily On-Line Newsletter
To subscribe (no cost):
http://www.feat.org/FEATNews

This on-line daily newsletter provides features and breaking news in the world of autism.

NAARRATIVE
Published by the National Alliance for Autism Research (NAAR)
99 Wall Street
Research Park
Princeton, NJ 08540
Tel: (609)-430-9160
(888)-777-NAAR
Fax: (609)-430-9163
www.naar.org

Our Voice
Published quarterly by the Autism Network International
P. O. Box 35448
Syracuse, NY 13235-5448
www.ani.autistics.org

PDD Newsletter

Published bimonthly by the Connecticut Autism Spectrum Resource Center, Inc.
300 East Rock Road
New Haven, CT 06511
Tel: (203)-787-3676
Fax: (203)-787-3676
www.CT-ASRC.org

Reporter

Published three times per year by the Indiana Institute on Disability and Community
The University Affiliated Program of Indiana
Indiana Resource Center for Autism
2853 East Tenth Street
Bloomington, IN 47408-2696
Tel: (812)-855-6508
Fax: (812)-855-9630

The MAAP

Published by MAAP (More Advanced Individuals with Autism, Asperger's Syndrome, and Pervasive Developmental Disorder)
Maap Services, Inc.
P. O. Box 254
Crown Point, IN 46308
Tel: (219)-662-1311
Fax: (219)-662-0638
www.maapservices.org

The Source
*Published quarterly by the Asperger Syndrome Coalition of the
United States (ASC-U.S.)*
P. O. Box 351268
Jacksonville Beach, FL 32235-1268
Tel: (866)-4-ASPRGR
www.asperger.org

Support Groups

Asperger Syndrome Coalition of the United States (ASC-U.S.)
P. O. Box 351268
Jacksonville Beach, FL 32235-1268
Tel: (866)-4-ASPRGR
www.asperger.org

Autism Network International
P. O. Box 35448
Syracuse, NY 13235-5448
www.ani.autistics.org

This organization is designed for and operated by individuals
with autism.

Autism Society of America (ASA)
7910 Woodmont Avenue, Suite 300
Bethesda, MD 20814-3067
Tel: (800)-3-AUTISM
(301)-657-0881
Fax: (301)-657-0869
www.autism-society.org

Families of Adults Afflicted with Asperger's Syndrome (FAAAS, Inc.)
P. O. Box 514
Centerville, MA 02632
www.faaas.org